Sharing Living Water

Evangelism as Caring Friendship

Steve Clapp and Sam Detwiler

**ANDREW
CENTER
RESOURCES**

Sharing Living Water
Evangelism as Caring Friendship

Steve Clapp and Sam Detwiler

Copyright © 1996 by LifeQuest. Published by **The Andrew Center**, 1451 Dundee Avenue, Elgin, Illinois 60120.

Biblical quotations, unless otherwise noted, are from the New Revised Standard Version of the Bible, copyrighted 1989 by the Division of Christian Education, National Council of Churches, and are used by permission.

ISBN 0-9637206-8-6

Manufactured in the United States of America

Contents

Rather than a traditional table of contents, we've chosen to include not only the chapter titles but also the core concept which is covered in each chapter. You will gain the most from this book if you read it completely through. If you are in a hurry, however, we recommend that, as a minimum, you read chapters one, two, four, five, six, eight, and nine.

This book is dedicated to:

- My wife, Floy Detwiler, and the kind people of the Nettle Creek Church of the Brethren who supported me with their encouragement, understanding, and prayers during the writing of this book. *Sam Detwiler*

- My wife, Sara Sprunger Clapp, and my mother, Mary Jo Clapp. They continue to write a book in my heart which nurtures and sustains me. *Steve Clapp*

We also extend our appreciation for the valuable contributions made to the production of this book by Paul Mundey, Barb Faga, Karen Carlson, Carolyn Egolf, Holly Carcione, Kristen Leverton, Jerry Peterson, and the staff of Evangel Press.

Introduction

If you are reading this page, you probably have chosen the Christian faith and are involved in the life of a local congregation. You should find concepts and ideas in *Sharing Living Water* which will increase your comfort in talking about your faith with others and in reaching out to others for Christ and the church. You'll find your own life enriched in the process, and you'll gain skills in listening and reaching out which should help you in many aspects of life.

You may, however, be one of the increasing numbers of people who embrace the Christian faith but currently reject involvement in a local congregation. If that is the case, you will still find guidance in more comfortably talking about your faith in ways which can enrich your life. We also hope you will gain enough perspective on how the church at its best should function that you will want to attempt connection with a local congregation. In spite of imperfections, the institutional church continues to be the primary setting in which most people experience the love and acceptance of the body of Christ and the motivation to reach out in words and action. Where that is not the case, we need, with God's help, to change it.

If you do not consider yourself a Christian, these pages should still help you talk about your own faith tradition or even lack of belief. And we hope these pages may increase your interest in learning more about the faith which motivated them.

This book has truly been a collaborative project. We worked together to develop the concept of the book and a detailed outline, and we exchanged manuscripts to give each other feedback. For those interested in such divisions: Steve is the primary author of chapters one, two, six, ten, and eleven. Sam is the primary author of chapters four, five, seven, eight, and nine. Both of us wrote substantial blocks for chapters three and twelve.

"When the poor and needy seek water and there is none, and their tongue is parched with thirst, I the Lord will answer them, I the God of Israel will not forsake them."

Isaiah 41:17

"'The water that I will give will become in them a spring of water gushing up to eternal life.'"

John 4:14

"They are like trees planted by streams of water, which yield their fruit in its season, and their leaves do not wither, in all that they do, they prosper."

Psalm 1:3

Chapter One
Death, Sex, and Faith

Concept: Many of us are uncomfortable sharing our faith and inviting others to church. The discomfort is normal; but if we care for people and our Lord, we need to develop natural, nonmanipulative ways to let others know what Christ and the church have done in our lives. That kind of sharing does wonderful things for others and transforms our own lives.

"My oncologist keeps telling me to think of myself as fighting a battle with the cancer cells in my body and to form a vision of the sick cells dying and the healthy cells living. That may be a good strategy for some of his younger patients, but it's beginning to sound ridiculous to this old woman. Look at me."

She held up an emaciated hand for just a moment, stared at it as though it belonged to someone else, and then let it flop back on the bed. "Skin and bones. That's about all that's left. I ask most people not even to hold my hand because they squeeze too hard even though they're trying to be gentle."

Katherine was in her early seventies and had been diagnosed with cancer six months before this particular hospital conversation. She and her husband were deeply spiritual, caring people. I had frequently known them to show great kindness to others, usually acting in such a self-effacing way that the recipients of their generosity weren't even sure whom to thank. Katherine had also been responsible for a significant number of persons who had come to faith in Jesus Christ and joined the life of our congregation. Over the years, she had filled nearly every volunteer position in the church and also had served on the boards of many community social service agencies. Her life had made a difference. My heart ached for Katherine and her husband as her body continued deteriorating.

Neither of us said anything as she tilted her head toward the water glass. I picked the glass up, carefully put a hand behind her head to give her the support I had learned was needed, and let her take a few sips through the straw. Then she laid her head against the pillow and closed her eyes for a few moments.

I stepped back and waited. Just as I had decided that she had fallen asleep and that I should leave, she looked at me again and continued, "I'm going to die. You know that, don't you?" I nodded in agreement. "Good. At least you can admit it. I sometimes think the doctors and nurses and hospital staff view it as a negative reflection on them when a patient has the nerve to die. Well, I'm sorry, but God has designed life so that the ultimate failure rate for physicians is one hundred percent. We die. That's the way the plan works."

She swallowed a couple of times and coughed to clear her throat before going on. "Part of what makes it so hard is that we've all got these foolish things that we just don't talk about. Like sex. When you're young, people don't answer your questions. How do they expect you to learn about these things? I was terrified when I had my first period, thought I was going to die, because my parents hadn't been able to make themselves talk to me about a normal, wonderful part of life. I suppose it's a little better now, but it's not good. My children and grandchildren talk freely enough about sex in the media, but they aren't in the least comfortable talking about more personal aspects like their own birth control."

She swallowed again. "Death we only want to discuss in the most general terms. Not my death and how I feel about it. I feel as though I'm ready. My faith is stronger than ever, and I know Jesus is calling me home, to my real home. Some people don't feel ready to give me up, but it's time. I'm not winning this so-called battle against the cancer in my body."

We visited together for several minutes about her husband's concerns over her approaching death and about her own growing conviction that the time for her departure had come. Then she began sharing some of the ways in which she felt her own faith had grown.

"You know," she said, "we really don't talk about personal faith any better than we talk about death, not in our denomination. It should be the most important thing in our lives, but we feel awkward discussing it with anyone and certainly don't know how to talk about it with someone outside the church.

"When I first began talking more comfortably with people about what my faith and the church mean to me, my husband actually became irritated. He thought that people outside of the church might think I was trying to get them to develop faith in God or to come to our congregation, as though that would be a bad thing. Of course that's been twenty years ago now. I wasn't actually trying to evangelize anyone, but I probably should have been. He wouldn't have thought of complaining if I had been trying to get someone to join the library association or the humane society.

"These days he's as comfortable as I am talking about personal faith." She swallowed again. "I understand why people feel reluctant to talk about what they believe. It feels like a very personal thing, and most of us don't feel especially secure about our ability to express what we believe so that it won't sound silly or superstitious to someone else.

"The door–to–door visits of Jehovah's Witnesses, the four spiritual laws approach, and religious tract distribution are what we think of when witnessing or faith–sharing is mentioned. Most Christians don't want to be identified with those approaches. I shouldn't group them into a single category, but that's how it comes across to a lot of the people outside of the church. The Jehovah's Witnesses I've known are very sincere people. The four spiritual laws have brought many people to Christ, but I think they also increasingly turn off large numbers. Religious tracts can have a place if they're truly written to speak to people today, but most of the tracts I've seen aren't very impressive.

"No one wants to be written-off as a religious crackpot, so it's easier not to talk about what a person believes. And of course I don't think we should be trying to impose our faith on our Jewish friends – well, we shouldn't try to impose it on anyone. That's rude and arrogant; and besides that, it simply doesn't work."

Katherine stopped to rest her voice, and I gave her another drink of water. Then I invited her to continue talking about her faith if she felt up to it.

She did: "Sharing the faith grows out of a person's love for Christ and for others, but I think there are very personal rewards for doing it. When I started talking about my faith with people who weren't in the church was precisely when I truly began to understand what I believed and to ask questions of my own faith. Once you learn to break the habit of not saying anything about it, it's actually easy to get people to visit about God. We're all pulled toward God. I started to learn marvelous things about the faith of other people, including a lot of people I had never thought about as being particularly religious. It's like my whole life was enriched. And relationships with other people are transformed when you start praying for their well-being, including their relationships with God.

"When people come in here and say something about my having such a strong faith, I ask them how they feel about their own faith. When they realize I'm serious about the question, they start talking; and the experience is tremendous. It's actually easier to make the step to talking about personal faith than to talking about sex and death, if you just get past that first step."

Talking about Our Faith

Katherine died a couple of days after that conversation. The accuracy of her observations has stayed with me. While persons in some denominational traditions are comfortable talking about their faith, sharing that faith with others, and inviting others to church, substantial numbers of people are at least as uncomfortable discussing their faith as discussing sex or death.

Many of us in North America are more comfortable talking about death than we were at the time of my visit with Katherine. Professionals have continued to increase our awareness of the relationship between death and life and of the importance of talking about death. That is perhaps especially important for those like Katherine who are about to die. As Elisabeth Kübler-Ross expressed in her classic book *On Death and Dying*, there is a need for people to "talk about death and dying as an intrinsic part of life just as they do not hesitate to mention when someone is expecting a baby" [p. 125].

The widespread publicity given to AIDS and to abortion issues has forced more conversations about at least some aspects of sexuality on our society. Of course we still have far to go in providing the information and the values which young people, in particular, need to make healthy decisions in this area.

People have always been more open to discussing death and sexuality in general terms than in specific or personal terms. The same is true for religious faith. Vast numbers of us may discuss religious topics like angels, heaven, and hell in a general way; but we are not comfortable talking about our personal faith, verbally witnessing to our faith with persons outside of the Christian community, or even inviting nonmembers to share in worship or in other church activities.

This reality has had significant impact on the growth and decline of many congregations. Repeated studies have made it clear that the vast majority of people visit a congregation for the first time because they were invited to do so by a friend, family member, coworker, neighbor, or acquaintance. That reality remains true in spite of the impact of television evangelism, direct mail, and other approaches to sharing the faith and interesting people in a particular local congregation. The pie chart on the next page shows this reality in a dramatic way.

The full caption for the largest slice of the chart should be "friend, family member, coworker, neighbor, or well-known acquaintance." Growing congregations almost always have many members who are inviting persons outside the church to come to church activities, and growing congregations are also more likely than declining ones to have members who actively share their faith with persons outside the church community. For more information about the other categories shown in the chart, refer to The Andrew Center publication *Overcoming Barriers to Church Growth*. Information on obtaining that book can be found in the *Resources* chapter of this book.

% of People Who Visit a Church Because Of

■	A Crusade
▨	Radio-TV Ad
☐	Newspaper
☐	Drive-By
■	Yellow Pages
▨	Brochure
☐	Music
▨	Sunday school
▦	Support Group
▨	Other Program
▥	Personal Problem
▨	Pastor
▨	Friend

From *Overcoming Barriers to Church Growth* [Andrew Center Resources, p. 48]

Comfort in Sharing and Inviting

A study begun in 1995 and continued in 1996 has examined attitudes and practices of active congregational members in local churches which are growing in contrast to those in local churches which are staying the same in membership or declining. The results show some clear differences between growing congregations and declining congregations in terms of the comfort of members in talking about their faith and in inviting others to worship and other activities. The following chart summarizes a few of the findings from that study:

14

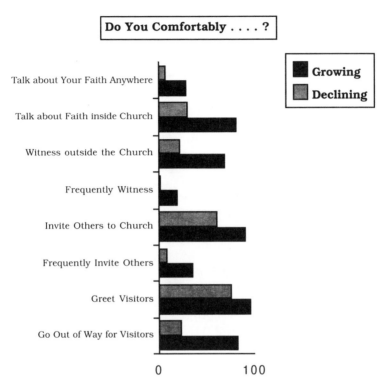

Do You Comfortably . . . . ?

- Talk about Your Faith Anywhere
- Talk about Faith inside Church
- Witness outside the Church
- Frequently Witness
- Invite Others to Church
- Frequently Invite Others
- Greet Visitors
- Go Out of Way for Visitors

■ **Growing**
□ **Declining**

0   100

Part of this information first appeared in *Evangelism: Good News or Bad News?* [Andrew Center Resources]

The study involved churches of many different denominational traditions and geographical settings. Congregations which are essentially staying the same in membership were included in the "declining" category. The bars indicate the percentage of respondents in growing and declining congregations who felt comfortable:

- *talking about their faith with anyone and in any setting unless doing so is clearly prohibited.* While those who were active members in growing congregations were more likely than those in declining congregations to indicate comfort in doing so, the reality is that the majority of persons in both congregational categories are not comfortable discussing their faith in all settings. This

15

probably does not as much reflect reluctance to share the faith as an awareness that some settings are not appropriate. The percentage agreeing was 28% in growing churches and only 7% in ones which are holding even or declining.

- *talking about their personal faith with others in class or group settings of the congregation.* Obviously comfort levels were far greater for conversations which take place in the local church. Without any question, the subject matter is appropriate to the setting; and people very likely already know one another. Eighty-one percent of those in growing congregations feel comfortable with this kind of sharing in contrast to 30% in declining congregations.

- *personally witnessing to their faith with at least one person outside the congregation during the last few weeks.* The percentage agreeing with the statement (69% in growing congregations and 22% in declining ones) obviously is lower than for those comfortable talking about their faith in congregational settings, but it is not as much lower as one might expect. The next item is more revealing.

- *personally witnessing on a frequent basis to persons outside the congregation, having done so in excess of a dozen times over the past year.* When asked to think of personal witnessing or faith-sharing actually done over a longer period of time, the percentages drop dramatically. Nineteen percent of those in growing congregations indicate having done so, in contrast to only 2% of those in declining congregations.

- *personally inviting, during the last few weeks, at least one person outside the congregation to participate in worship or other church activities.* The percentages climb rather dramatically for the active church members who responded to this item, with 91% of those in growing growing congregations and 61% of those in declining congregations indicating agreement. The next item, however, shows a somewhat different view.

- *personally inviting, on at least a dozen occasions over the past year, persons outside the congregation to participate in worship or other church activities.* The percentage of agreement drops to 35% for growing congregations and plummets all the way to 8% in declining congregations.

• *personally extending greetings to persons who are visitors to their congregation, whether they know those persons or not.* The percentages here are very high, with 96% of those in growing congregations and 76% of those in declining congregations agreeing. Once again, however, note what happens as the standard is raised slightly.

• *personally going out of their way to extend greetings to visitors, even if that means separating for a time from church friends in order to seek out the newcomers.* The percentage dips to 83% for those in growing congregations, but it dives all the way to 23% for declining congregations.

All the percentages of agreement are probably higher than a truly random assortment of congregations would be, since the interest of churches in participating in the study was certainly related to their desire to improve their outreach. Congregations serious about improving outreach, even if they are currently only holding even on membership or actually declining, are more likely to have tried various strategies to encourage members to share their faith and to invite other persons to church than are congregations which are not yet struggling seriously with such issues.

Think about the significance of the numbers. Only 8% of those in declining congregations are frequently inviting someone to attend church activities, and only 2% of those in such congregations are involved in any frequent sharing of their faith with persons outside the church. In fact, this author's experience is that there are large numbers of churches, not participating in a study like the one just described, in which literally no one ever invites someone else to attend worship or another church activity. Think of the impact on congregations around North America if those numbers could be dramatically improved!

17

Reasons for Not Reaching Out

But how do those of us who do not feel comfortable talking about our faith and inviting others to church begin doing so on a frequent or regular basis? Most of us can identify at least some of the reasons for not reaching out:

The Top Ten Reasons for Not Reaching Out

- "I'm afraid I'll look foolish if I talk about my faith."
- "I don't want to use a canned formula like 'the four spiritual laws.'"
- "I don't know how to bring it up in conversation."
- "It seems like too personal a topic."
- "I don't want to admit it, but I'm afraid of growth. I like the church as it is right now, and I'm not sure I want new people."
- "I'm not as firm as I want to be in my own faith, so it terrifies me to think about sharing it with another person."
- "I take the peace and justice emphasis of my denomination seriously, and I sometimes feel like there's a conflict between that and evangelism."
- "I'd like to share my faith, but I'm just too busy. There isn't enough time to do it."
- "I've heard people say so many negative things about the church and the Christian faith, that the idea of sharing the faith or inviting someone to church doesn't seem realistic to me."
- "I think there's so much wrong with my church that it wouldn't be right to ask someone to join. I need to feel excited about my church before asking someone else to be a part of it."

All of those statements were in fact shared by substantial numbers of persons who participated in the study from which the preceding chart was taken. While persons in growing congregations contributed to the above list, they did not do so with the same frequency as persons in declining congregations.

What makes the difference between persons feeling comfortable sharing their faith and inviting others to church and persons wishing to avoid doing so? The major difference seems to come at the point of actual instruction from the church. Persons in the study were asked to indicate if they had received some kind of instruction from the church in how to share their faith with others and in how to invite others to worship and other church events:

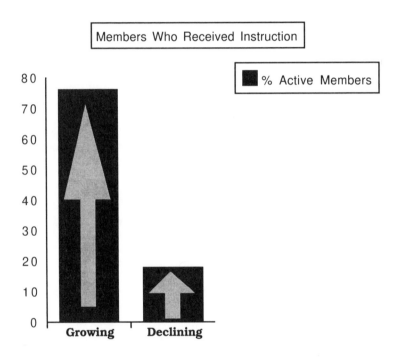

Members Who Received Instruction

% Active Members

Growing   Declining

Growing congregations are far more likely to provide instruction in faith-sharing and invitational evangelism than are declining congregations. That variable emerged as far more significant than any theological or denominational differences between growing and declining congregations. Because so many of us are not naturally comfortable sharing our personal faith and inviting others to church, the opportunity to gain practice, skill, and experience in doing so can make a difference.

Personal Enrichment from Faith-Sharing

Many of our congregation members, especially in mainline Protestant and Anabaptist churches, remain insecure about sharing their faith, sometimes even within church settings. Richard Kew and Roger White described the situation in *New Millennium, New Church* in this way: "By and large, American mainline churches enter the 1990s crippled by a phobia about the concept of evangelism" [p. 101].

A similar perspective is shared by Tony Campolo and Gordon Aeschliman in *Fifty Ways You Can Share Your Faith*: "The very idea of evangelism has been polluted with bad preaching, guilt trips, and goofy schemes that almost no one feels comfortable employing – and that offend more often than they draw people to Christ" [pp. 9-10]. The phobia is alive and well in many of our congregations. The cost of that phobia is not only lower levels of membership, attendance, and financial support but also impoverished spiritual lives on the part of our active church members.

Those of us who are reticent about sharing our faith are often inclined to be critical of persons who seem to do so with a formula-like approach. Campus Crusade for Christ's four spiritual laws have become well-known as an approach for saving souls. As effective as that strategy has been for many people, it also turns off vast numbers of Christians and causes some outside the faith to run for cover. In our haste to be judgmental of such approaches, however, we may fail to recognize the benefits that faith–sharing brings.

Katherine was very clear about the gains for her own life which came as she began to feel more comfortable talking about personal faith with other people. While there are clear scriptural admonitions that we share our faith with others, the strongest motivation for talking about what we believe may in fact be in the personal gain that we experience as a result. For example:

- Talking about our faith pushes us to think about what we believe in different ways. While words are certainly not adequate to describe many dimensions of religious experience, the search for words clarifies our thinking. We also begin asking important questions concerning our faith.

- We learn from others in the process. Talking with people about the faith should be an act of dialogue – in which we hear their concerns and ideas as well as express our own. In fact, the approach to be discussed in this book is one which places far greater emphasis on listening than on speaking. This kind of interaction with others always enriches our lives and deepens our own faith. We do have a lot to learn, not only from others who are involved in the life of the church, but also from persons who are completely outside the church and who have been turned off by the way Christianity has been presented to them in the past.

- Developing a concern about the spiritual lives of others is just as important as developing a concern about their physical or emotional well–being. As we develop that concern, we find ourselves thinking about others with greater caring and understanding.

- Praying for the overall well-being of others, including their spiritual lives, should be an integral part of faith–sharing. Those prayers draw us as individuals closer to God and also deepen our understanding of others.

- Though our motivation for talking about our faith and the church should not simply be one of working for congregational growth, it is nevertheless very satisfying when our efforts result in people developing a new or deepened relationship with Jesus Christ and becoming active in the life of the church.

Attitudes as Barriers

You and I are actually living in a time of greatly heightened interest in spiritual matters in North America. Books on the spiritual life are selling so well that some major publishers have added religious publishing divisions, and *Publishers Weekly*, the trade journal of the publishing industry, has actually added a new publication just on religious releases. Many people outside the church and even a few inside the church, however, are more negative toward the church as an institution than past generations have been.

Many of us in the church feel threatened by trends in society, and it's easy for us to become focused on a view of the church as a "safe haven" from the dangers of the larger world. While there are important ways in which the church is indeed a safe haven, such a view can keep us from developing healthy relationships with persons outside of the church. Just as persons outside of the church may be turned off by an approach to evangelism which seems filled with gimmicks or based on an overly simplistic view, those of us who embrace the Christian faith are sometimes so turned off by some characteristics of persons outside of the church that we feel unable or unwilling to develop relationships with them. For example, many Christians feel negatively toward:

- Persons who use excessive amounts of profanity.
- Persons who have drinking or illegal drug problems.
- Males and females living together but not married.
- Homosexuals.
- Unmarried parents.

There are also persons outside of the church, of course, who are turned off by persons in categories like those just described. Some of us probably need to spend more time studying the numerous biblical passages which warn us about judgment, such as these words of our Lord:

> *How can you say to your neighbor, "Let me take the speck out of your eye," while the log is in your own eye?*
> **Matthew 7:4**

Forming judgments about the worth or depth of other people on the basis of one or two characteristics separates us from relationships which might well be meaningful for us and which also could make a difference for those who have rejected the church as an institution.

Donald C. Posterski in *Reinventing Evangelism* warns: "The lack of acceptance by Christians of those who are not yet followers of Jesus is one of the major obstacles to fruitful witnessing. Failure on the part of Christians to extend acceptance to nonbelievers shuts down relationships before they have an opportunity to develop. The wrong signal is sent and the door is shut" [p. 72].

In some respects, views of the institutional church have become harsher than in some past generations, especially among those who reject the church but also among many of us who continue to be active in the life of the church. Focus group studies of persons who are unchurched reveal that many of those persons do not feel especially positive about any of the denominational families. The classification which follows is obviously too simplistic, but consider the summaries of the views of unchurched persons toward congregations in these categories:

Evangelical congregations are generally recognized as fast-growing by the unchurched but are often viewed as being more interested in a person's spiritual scalp, volunteer hours, and money than in the person as an individual. Pastors of these churches are viewed as being very hard-working and very driven by their desire for numerical success. These congregations are of greatest interest to persons who want a very well-defined belief system, which is not always attractive to those outside the church.

Fundamentalist and conservative congregations are often viewed by those outside the church as hot–beds of right wing politics. Focus groups have revealed that many outside of the church feel that fundamentalist churches have a creed in addition to their officially-stated doctrines. The unchurched often feel that you shouldn't join one of these churches unless you're anti-abortion, anti-welfare, anti-gay, and pro-Republican. The unchurched see these congregations being of interest primarily to persons who want carefully defined beliefs and who share a particular set of political views.

Mainline Protestant congregations are viewed by the unchurched as being more open to diversity of belief and lifestyle than evangelical or fundamentalist churches but are also seen as stodgy and not very open to change. The pastors of these congregations come across as well-educated and caring but not necessarily able to help with spiritual issues. The unchurched see these congregations as being of interest primarily to persons who are not on the right wing of the political spectrum and who appreciate not having doctrine shoved down their throats.

23

Anabaptist congregations are very often not well understood by those outside of those churches, including by persons who are in Protestant denominations. The unchurched who have had some experience with Mennonite, General Conference Mennonite, Church of the Brethren, Brethren Church, and Brethren in Christ congregations generally view these churches as closed circles with the assumption being that you are basically born into the denomination. The unchurched see these churches being of interest primarily to those familiar with the Anabaptist peace and justice heritage. That heritage had to be explained to most of those in the focus groups.

Roman Catholic congregations are better known than most Anabaptist ones and some Protestant ones, but they are not necessarily better understood or better thought of by those on the outside. In focus groups, many misconceptions appeared concerning the role of the pope, the conduct of priests, and several aspects of parish life. The official positions of the Roman Catholic Church on birth control and women in the priesthood constitute significant barriers to many of the unchurched.

Is the Church Necessary?

The preceding are certainly overly-simplified summaries of significant focus group study, but the message is clear. The church as an institution is not especially favorably viewed by those who are not part of its life. Many of the statements of focus group participants are based on misinformation and are unfair to the church, but those statements reflect how large numbers of people actually feel. Television evangelists, media publicity about church scandals, bad experiences from childhood, and negative comments from friends and family members who are active in the church have all contributed to the kinds of views just shared. [For more information on the focus group study summarized above, see the *Resources* section.]

In trying to create safe harbors from the larger society, many of our churches have resisted change to excessive degrees. In *Illuminata*, Marianne Williamson shares an insightful perspective: "Secularized organized religions have become, in many cases, as calcified as other institutions that form the structure of our modern world. That's why they are accepted here, and also why they are rejected. Our religious institutions have far too often become handmaidens of the status quo, while the genuine religious experience is anything but that. True religion is by nature disruptive of what has been, giving birth to the eternally new within us" [p. 31]. Thus we find ourselves with churches which need to change in order to reach those on the outside but with members who want desperately for the church to stay the same.

The last decade has brought a growing confidence among many people that one can be a good Christian without being part of an organized church. This perspective flows from a more negative view of the institutional church and from a realization that no single church or denominational system fully captures every aspect of the nature of God.

In The Andrew Center publication *Fifty Ways to Reach Young Singles, Couples, and Families*, data was reported from a study of how young adults, both members and nonmembers, view the church in contrast to older adults who are members. The study made it clear that a great many young adults are not convinced that one must be a member of a local church in order to be a Christian. This is true not only for those who aren't involved in a church but also for many who are thoroughly involved. Older members of the church tend to view the local congregation as part of the body of Christ and cannot conceive of being a Christian in isolation. No doubt this difference in perspective has a lot to do with the lower numbers of young adults who actually join a local church. The responses which follow are all given as percentages of persons in each category expressing agreement with the statements:

Statement	19-35 Nonm.	19-35 Memb.	36 & Older Memb.
The local church is too much like an institution or a bureaucracy.	68%	61%	30%
You can be a good Christian even though you don't belong to a local church.	86%	73%	21%

As the statistics indicate, increasing numbers of people are making a distinction between the church as an institution and the Christian faith. As the focus group results made clear, some of the negative judgments on the church are unfair and are based on misinformation, but that is part of the reality of our times. The amount of misinformation both about the church as an organization and about Jesus Christ is staggering. Posterski warns: "For many in North America, familiarity with Jesus and language about him stands in the way of a deeper spiritual experience with him" [*Reinventing Evangelism*, p. 86].

Such challenges push us to think about not only what we believe and what the church declares but also about how we are truly perceived in society. When we think about sharing the faith, we should be aware that we will often be doing so to people who have serious doubts about Christianity and who have even more serious doubts about the local church. What do those of us who are Christian and who see ourselves as part of Christ's body, the church, have to offer the rest of society?

Living Water

We cannot live without water; but in our modern culture, we are far more tempted to take its availability for granted than were people in biblical times. It's not surprising that Scripture contains so many references to water and that longing for God is compared to thirst for water. Consider the following passages:

Genesis 1:10. *God called the dry land earth, and the waters that were gathered together he called seas. And God saw that it was good.* God created a world in which water is absolutely essential. Water makes up two-thirds of our bodies!

John 4:13-14. *Jesus said to her: "Everyone who drinks of this water will be thirsty again, but those who drink of the water that I will give them will never be thirsty. The water that I will give will become in them a spring of water gushing up to eternal life."* Jesus had started the conversation by requesting a drink of water from the woman at the well. That request would have surprised her since most Jewish men would not have accepted a drink from a woman of Samaria. The water Jesus offered was for all people.

Exodus 15:23. *When they came to Marah, they could not drink the water of Marah because it was bitter.* Moses seeks help from God, and the water is made sweet. Just as water intended for physical nourishment can become polluted and unable to be safely or pleasantly consumed, so also can our presentations of the living water of Christ become filled with bitterness and judgment. Then people will not accept what is offered because they do not believe it will improve their lives.

Amos 5:22-24. *Even though you offer me your burnt offerings and grain offerings, I will not accept them. . . . Take away from me the noise of your songs; I will not listen to the melody of your harps. But let justice roll down like waters, and righteousness like an everflowing stream.* Flowing water becomes in this passage a strong symbol for justice. If we do not stand for a just society, if we are not willing to side with the oppressed, we should not be surprised that our worship becomes unacceptable and that our witness becomes tainted. Sharing living water is not just a matter of verbal witness but of our willingness to put Christ first in all things.

Matthew 5:6. *Blessed are those who hunger and thirst for righteousness, for they will be filled.* God has placed a hunger and a thirst deep within us which can only be met by accepting Christ and seeking to lead a life of discipleship.

Psalm 1:3. *They are like trees planted by streams of water, which yield their fruit in its season, and their leaves do not wither. In all that they do, they prosper.* Those who depend on God are like trees planted by streams of water for they are revitalized.

John 1:43-51 doesn't use the analogy of water for the eternal life which Christ offers, but this passage about the call of Philip and Nathanael shows evangelism at its most basic level. Philip responds to the call "Follow me." He finds his friend Nathanael and shares the good news with him: "We have found him about whom Moses in the law and also the prophets wrote, Jesus son of Joseph from Nazareth." Nathaniel is skeptical: "Can anything good come out of Nazareth?" Philip doesn't give him a lengthy argument (at least as far as the text indicates), but he invites him to "Come and see."

Faith-sharing should always take place in the context of a relationship, such as that between Philip and Nathanael. Faith-sharing involves sharing living water, for which people long, rather than engaging in doctrinal arguments or in powerful persuasive techniques.

A Comfortable Process for Faith-Sharing

While we may not seem to receive as clear messages from our Lord as came to Philip in the passage just considered, we should seek natural opportunities for faith-sharing. That's how we can be comfortable with the process and the only way we are likely to be effective!

I hope you don't gain the impression that we are intending to put down approaches to faith-sharing like the four spiritual laws or people who hand out tracts. Such strategies have had significant impact on many people. Those are also strategies, however, that are uncomfortable for huge numbers of Christian people and which are a decided turn-off in much of today's society. As this book proceeds, we'll be helping you develop a stance toward life, faith, and other people which makes inviting others to church and talking with others about your faith a natural extension of who you are and of your relationships with those persons.

A couple of cautions should be considered before moving to the next chapter. Thomas Moore, in *Meditations*, shares this perspective: "I've never had the impression that Jesus or the Buddha were proselytizers. It simply wasn't their style to run membership campaigns or even to 'network'" [p. 30]. We must approach others with genuine respect. "Soul respects another's failure to find perfection, resistance to enlightenment, sheer ignorance of absolute truth, misguided attachments, and unrelenting meandering" [p. 30]. It's not our goal to manipulate anyone or to do anything obnoxious. It's extremely important to respect the right of others to see the world differently than we do and to express their beliefs differently than we choose to do. We are called to share the faith we have received; we are not called to impose it.

Another caution: our motivation for sharing our faith must be something other than or at least more than the church's being in trouble. Many of our churches are in trouble in terms of membership, attendance, volunteer workers, and finances – but rescuing the church is not the best reason to reach out to others. Perhaps God has in fact decided to use the decline in many of our churches as an opportunity to motivate us to share our faith and do what we should have been all along. Living water is meant to be shared – not to be hoarded. Faith–sharing at its best, by God's grace, is an experience of mutuality from which both parties gain.

The basic process which we'll be sharing in this book can be summarized in this way:

We can comfortably relate our faith in Christ to others and invite others into the life of the church through a process of:
- Forming genuine friendships.
- Listening to the needs of our friends and learning to ask deeper questions.
- Caring for our friends and showing that care in words and actions.
- Telling in our own words how Christ and the church have made a difference in our lives, building not so much on our strength or wisdom as on our weakness.
- Inviting others into the life of the congregation.
- Helping those who join the church become fully incorporated into the body of Christ.
- Recognizing that it is Christ who saves and that we must respect where others are in openness to Christ and the church.

☞ *But . . .*

> *What if you aren't yet convinced? What if the possibility of talking about your faith with others, especially with persons outside the church, feels so uncomfortable that you can't imagine yourself doing it? Be patient with yourself. The only commitment you need to make at this time is to finish the book! You will learn things about communication, about relationships, and*

*about people which will enrich your life whether
or not you decide to actively share your faith.*

*Many people who are church active and
reading this book will find inviting others to
church a more comfortable starting point than
verbal witnessing to their faith. There are plenty
of options. Read the book, try the suggested
activities that feel comfortable to you, pray,
and see what happens!*

Some Things to Try

1. If you are comfortable doing so, talk with a good friend in the church or in the community about your initial responses to this chapter. What new insights, if any, did you receive from this chapter? What possibilities are exciting to you? What anxieties, if any, do you have?

2. Visit with one other person, perhaps a member of your family or a church friend, about a time when God or the church has had especially significant impact on your life. Share what that impact has been, and listen to experiences the other person has had.

3. If you have a friend who is not involved in a local congregation, tell that person you are reading a book about ways to share the faith with others and to invite others to church. Tell your friend that understanding why many people reject the church is very important to your gaining the most from the book. Ask your friend to share some of the reasons for which he or she has chosen not to be active in a congregation. Don't share criticisms or act defensively about what the person says. You may gain a great deal of perspective by listening to his or her observations.

Chapter Two
The Meaning of Friendship

Concept: Friendship, rooted in genuine caring rather than manipulation, is the most natural relationship for sharing the faith and inviting others to church.

The telephone rang as I was sitting down for dinner. My mother had been experiencing health problems, so I wasn't comfortable simply letting the answering machine receive the call. "This is Steve."

"Steve, it seems like a long time since we visited."

Uh. Duh. I felt vaguely familiar with the voice but couldn't place it. "I'm sorry, but I'm not recognizing your voice tonight."

"My fault. That's the problem with being the one making the call. You always assume the other person knows who you are. This is your friend Pete."

Pete? Someone I visited with during a series of workshops I'd recently conducted? Someone I met at the Christmas party hosted by the company for which my wife works? Someone I knew years ago? There was a Pete in some of my business classes in graduate school, but I hadn't heard from him in years. Maybe a member of a church I'd pastored – several Petes began coming to mind. Which Pete? "Oh, hi, Pete." I felt stupid. "How are things going for you?"

"Thanks for asking. I don't think anyone else has asked today. Anyway, it's been a great day for me – actually a great week. I hope you've had a good day."

I still couldn't place this person. "It's been a good day, but dinner is on the table. Could I take your phone number and give you a call later tonight?" Maybe the area code would give me a clue.

"Sure, Steve, no problem. Tell you what, I'll call back in a couple of hours. There are a few additional benefits to our term insurance policies that I want to talk with you about."

Pete. Yes, I remembered Pete then. He had called a couple of months earlier to pitch a term life insurance policy to me. I was getting ready to go to the airport when he called that time. He had asked if he could call back the next week, and I had declined, saying that it was a busy month. He had suggested that he try me again in a couple of months, and I'd grunted a hurried, "Oh, okay, I suppose," as I hung up the phone and headed out the door.

Friendship

So my friend Pete called again in the hope of selling me insurance. I like people, but one hurried phone conversation about insurance does not constitute "friendship," at least not by my understanding of the concept.

In many ways the concept of friendship seems to have been cheapened in our society, which seems filled with almost countless superficial relationships and with the tendency for friendship to be used as a marketing concept. Yet people are still desperately hungry for the real thing, for relationships that truly have meaning, and for people on whom they can count even when things aren't going well.

It's certainly true that the label "friendship" can be applied to many different kinds of relationships. It cannot, in my opinion, be stretched to include my relationship with any telephone solicitors I've yet encountered – including some who have been very pleasant people.

The most basic dictionary definitions of friendship include the concepts of knowing, liking, and trusting the person who is the friend. The depth of that knowing, liking, and trusting, of course, varies. We experience:

- New friendships with persons we have known for only a short period of time but whom we find likable and, insofar as we have had opportunity to relate to them, trustworthy.

- Friendships of a few years duration with persons we have met at school, work, church, or other settings. The difference between friendship and acquaintance relates at least in part to how much we like and are inclined to trust the other person.

- Friendships of many years duration with persons we encounter frequently through work, church, or community activities. We feel that we know these persons well and generally consider them reliable.

- Friendships of many years duration with persons we encounter only infrequently and who may even live a significant distance from us. We often invest significant effort in maintaining contact and at least occasionally getting together, but we also have the confidence that the friendship will still be strong even if months or years have passed since our last conversation.

- Friendships with that very small number of persons who have proven themselves completely trustworthy no matter what the situation. These are persons for whom we have strong affection and may even consider as part of our families.

Of course the preceding categories may have significant overlap; and friends, almost by definition, can't be neatly categorized. But they are important, and we hunger for them. In one LifeQuest study of young adults, almost all who participated listed the "desire for more friends" as one of the major needs in their lives.

The Impact of Friendship

In *Is There Anything I Can Do?*, Sol Gordon writes: "*Friendship* is a rather ordinary word, but it carries extraordinary significance in our lives" [p. xi]. Friends share with us in the joys of life. Friends pull us through the tough times. And friends provide us with the opportunity to show our love and reliability when they are in need of our help.

All of us who believe in Jesus Christ first learned of his life and of his desire to positively transform our lives through other persons. We do not learn about the faith in a vacuum. For most of us, faith comes alive in the words, actions, and influence of others. Over a period of time, we certainly do develop a deep and intimate direct relationship with God through prayer; but we are dependent on other persons for the concept of prayer.

In *Long Walk to Freedom*, Nelson Mandela shares this perspective on how the Christian faith came alive for him: "For me, Christianity was not so much a system of beliefs as it was the powerful creed of a single man: Reverend Matyolo. For me, his powerful presence embodied all that was alluring in Christianity." Through that man's influence, Mandela came to see the profound impact that Christ and the church had on African society at that time. "I saw that virtually all of the achievements of Africans seemed to have come about through the missionary work of the Church. The mission schools trained the clerks, the interpreters, and the policemen, who at the time represented the height of African aspirations" [p. 19].

What we do does make a difference. We don't have to convey the powerful presence of a Reverend Matyolo to our friends in order to have influence on them – kindness, gentleness, and consistency of concern carry weight which is just as great. If the quality of our relationships with others is solid, they will always be open to talking with us about important concerns, including religious faith. If our relationships are shallow and if we are unreliable, then others will not be interested in what we have to say.

The tests of friendship often come with problems. Sol Gordon tells of a man carrying a heavy load because of criminal acts by a mentally ill son: "The story was splashed across the front page of a local paper. Just when he needed his friends and associates the most, they began avoiding him" [p. 23]. He felt betrayed by people with whom he felt relationships were solid. Of course, people often are uncertain concerning what to say about such a situation, but it wasn't even necessary for friends to comment on the son's offense in order to share some considerate words with the father. Certainly a friend could say:

- "You must be going through a very difficult time. I'm really at a loss for words, but I want you to know that I care. I don't want to pry, but I'd be glad to sit down and talk if it would help you to share some of your feelings."

- "I'm sure I can't imagine what it's like to have the burdens which are on you right now. I do care about you and about your son. I'll be keeping you in my prayers, and I'd be glad to do anything else that would be of help to you."

In future chapters, we'll talk more specifically about ways to respond to awkward situations. **What we say, however, is often not nearly as important as that we take the time to reach out.**

The faith–sharing that we do, in fact, should generally be specifically related to situations in our own lives or in the lives of our friends. Such conversations are far more likely to have impact than simply approaching people and beginning to "witness." Our faith–sharing should never be imposed on others.

I wouldn't describe myself as a "frequent flier," but I do travel enough to have had several interesting airplane conversations. I often make flights exchanging only a few superficial words with those sitting near me on the plane, but there have been a few occasions when the conversations have had remarkable depth. The opportunity to talk to a perfect stranger, whom one never expects to see again, will occasionally cause a person to be surprisingly open. Such experiences, what I sometimes call the "airplane phenomenon," are, however, the exception. Most conversations of depth happen with persons we know very well – our friends.

Jonathan, David, and the Samaritan

The Old Testament friendship of Jonathan and David stands as one of the strongest examples of a close bond between two persons to be found in Scripture. Theirs was a friendship which was unquestionably grounded in God. In **1 Samuel 20:8b**, the relationship is described as a "sacred covenant." Then in verse 42 of the same chapter, Jonathan says to David: "Go in peace, since both of us have sworn in the name of the Lord, saying, The Lord shall be between me and you, and between my descendants and your descendants, forever." You may wish to read more about their friendship, especially in **1 Samuel 20**.

The New Testament parable of the Good Samaritan, **Luke 10:25-37**, tells us more about the scope of who should be included in the circle of our relationships. Just before Jesus told this well-known parable, he shared the two great commandments: "You shall love the Lord your God with all your heart, and with all your soul, and with all your strength, and with all your mind; and your neighbor as yourself" [v.27].

Then the lawyer asked Jesus: "And who is my neighbor?" [v.29]. To answer that question, Jesus told the story of the Good Samaritan. The parable was no doubt especially directed to that lawyer and to religious leaders who had great respect for priests and Levites. The priests were the religious leaders of highest rank, and the Levites were what we might call their lay associates. But the priest and the Levite passed the injured man without helping.

Many of the Jewish people who would have heard this parable disliked the Samaritan people. A contemporary version of the parable might have made this figure a black person, a white person, an Hispanic, a Korean, or another ethnic category, depending on the audience. The Samaritan provides the moral example for the parable, for he is the one who does what is right for the stranger. The stranger is to be treated as a neighbor. If a stranger is to be treated with such compassion and at such expense, then consider how we should respond to persons we know, to our closest friends!

The parable conveys many different messages, but perhaps none more important than that Christ wants us to show justice and compassion to all people, including those we do not even know. It greatly expands the concept of neighbor, and with that the concept of friendship.

The truth is that most of us tend to form friendships with persons who are very much like ourselves. An exercise at the end of this chapter will ask you to assess what categories are missing in your own circle of friends. As we broaden that circle, a topic which will be discussed more fully in future chapters, we expand our opportunities for helping others, enjoying new experiences, and sharing the faith.

The great commandments shared at the start of the parable of the Good Samaritan also carry another important message. If we are to love our neighbors as we love ourselves, then it is important for us to feel good about ourselves! If we are filled with self-hatred, self-contempt, or feelings of failure and make that the standard for how we treat others, we are not likely to form many good relationships.

Certainly Christ does not want us to be self-centered – the whole thrust of the gospel is on focusing our hearts and minds more fully on Christ and on other people. Healthy self-respect, however, is another matter. After all, we were all created in the image of God, which means we are persons of worth with significant gifts and abilities to be used in the world in which we have been placed. A healthy view of ourselves also helps prevent us from drifting into situations in which we become manipulated or abused by others.

If you find forming new friendships or maintaining existing ones especially difficult, consider the possibility that a low opinion of yourself may be part of the problem. Focusing on your own strengths and on your own relationship with Christ may be an important part of learning how to reach out to others.

Friendship and Evangelism

Many evangelistic strategies talk about ways to approach other persons with the Christian message. Concepts like the four spiritual laws are designed to make it easier to initiate a conversation about Christ with persons we do not know well. When the focus of our faith–sharing and church–inviting, however, is on friendship, then we are not under time pressure. We don't have to be in a hurry to share our faith, and we can wait for the natural, comfortable connecting points.

Of course it can also be easy to miss those connecting points. John Kramp talks about how easily we may miss the signals that another person wants to talk more about religious concerns or ultimate issues: "During conversation, a seeker may ask a question about the Bible or about church. Often, Christians dismiss the question as small talk and fail to probe what is on the person's mind" [p. 74]. Questions and observations about movies, music, television, politics, and any number of other topics can be natural connecting points in which faith-issues are raised.

It's also important to be aware of how crucial friendships are to the strength of the bonds that people have with local congregations. The chart on the next page compares several friendship measures for persons who are church members with a very high level of involvement (present at worship almost every week, solid contributors to church finances, and involved in one or more classes or groups in the church) with church members with a relatively low level of involvement (present at worship only a couple of times a year, nominal contributors, and not consistently involved in any class or group). The specific friendship measures shown on the chart as percentages are:

- I can name at least sixty people people who belong to or are active in my church.

- I joined this congregation because of a friendship with someone who was already a member. (Persons who literally grew up in the church to which they currently belong were excluded from the sample for this calculation, since their parents made the initial decision about their church home.)

- I would say that my closest friend is a member of my church.

- I have seven or more close friends in the church.

The contrast in responses to matters of friendship between those who have high involvement and those who have low involvement is striking. Friendship has a lot to do with people coming to the church for the first time, and it appears to have even more to do with persons staying in the church.

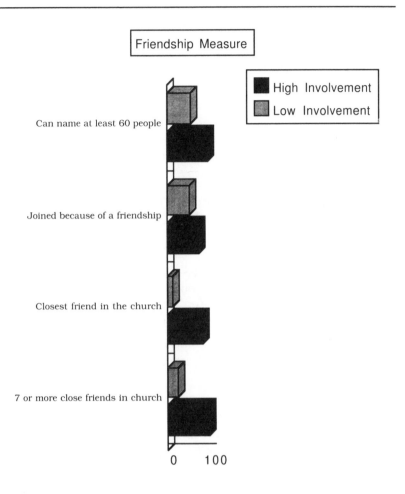

Friendship Measure

High Involvement
Low Involvement

Can name at least 60 people

Joined because of a friendship

Closest friend in the church

7 or more close friends in church

0   100

The phrase "friendship evangelism" has sometimes been applied to evangelistic strategies which consist of forming friendships just for the sake of getting someone to accept Christ and to start attending church. Some of the friendships formed in that way are very superficial and tend to disappear once the persons has actually joined the congregation. The friendship which is being discussed in this book has deeper roots than that. While forming a friendship with another person certainly can result in that person talking about religious faith with you, making a Christian commitment, and joining the church, the roots of the friendship should be deeper than searching for a spiritual scalp. Another person may justifiably feel manipulated when what appears to be genuine friendship disappears shortly after church membership is in place.

Some Things to Try

1. Complete the "Do Your Friends Include . . . ?" checklist at the end of this chapter. What would you gain from expanding your circle of friends?

2. Complete the "A Friend Is Someone Who . . ." exercise at the end of this chapter. Are there changes you would like to make in the way you relate to your friends? Are there changes you wish some of your friends would make?

3. In terms of your own life, who would play the part of the Samaritan if Jesus were to retell the parable for your benefit? What are the roots of your problems in accepting people with that particular characteristic?

4. If liking and accepting yourself is a significant problem, that can certainly make it difficult for you to relate positively to other people. Consider these self-acceptance ideas:

- Make a list of ten things you like about yourself.

- Start a regular exercise program if you aren't involved in one at the present time. Physical exercise helps us feel better about ourselves and generally improves our physical appearance, which helps self-image.

- Spend more time reading. Reading helps us learn, and learning almost always helps self-esteem.

- Do something creative. Build something with wood or other materials, paint something, write an essay or poem, sew something, cook something you haven't before, play a musical instrument, or do something else that involves you in the creative process.

- Pray more often. Prayer always strengthens our self-acceptance and our ability to reach out to others.

Do Your Friends Include. . . ?

Check each of the following if your circle of friends includes persons with that characteristic.

___ Persons from households with significantly lower incomes than your household.

___ Persons from households with significantly higher incomes than your household.

___ Persons who have disfiguring physical handicaps.

___ Persons who are learning disabled.

___ Persons of different ethnic backgrounds than your own.

___ Persons who have significantly less education than yourself.

___ Persons who have significantly more education than yourself.

___ Persons who are single parents.

___ Persons whose political views are very different from yours.

___ Persons who are not active in any local church.

___ Persons who appear not to have any religious faith.

___ Persons who have serious problems with depression.

___ Persons who have problems with alcohol or drugs.

___ Persons who have served time in jail or prison.

___ Persons who have been the victims of crime.

___ Persons who are significantly younger than you are.

___ Persons who are significantly older than you are.

___ Persons who have children at home.

___ Persons who have no children at home.

___ Persons who work in a totally different field than your own.

___ Other: _____

___ Other: _____

___ Other: _____

A Friend Is Someone Who . . .

*Place checks in the boxes to indicate which items are things **you** do in a close friendship and which things **your friends** do in their relationships with you. You may decide to focus on one particular friend. If you think a characteristic or activity doesn't belong on the list, scratch off that item. Add items if you wish.*

I Do This	My Friends Do This		Characteristic or Activity
❏	❏	1.	Ask what is wrong when my friend is upset.
❏	❏	2.	Admit to my friend when I'm wrong.
❏	❏	3.	Accept that my friend will have other friends in addition to me.
❏	❏	4.	Compliment my friend.
❏	❏	5.	Help my friend know when my faith affects my decisions.
❏	❏	6.	Never lie to my friend.
❏	❏	7.	Feel free to share opinions with my friend.
❏	❏	8.	Never say anything hurtful about my friend to others.
❏	❏	9.	Stand up to others for my friend.
❏	❏	10.	Talk about my faith with my friend.
❏	❏	11.	Stand by my friend when life is hard.
❏	❏	12.	Try to understand my friend's point of view when we disagree.
❏	❏	13.	Still like my friend even when he or she makes a mistake.
❏	❏	14.	Let my friend know what I appreciate about him or her.
❏	❏	15.	Warn my friend of possible trouble.
❏	❏	16.	Pray for my friend.
❏	❏	17.	Take the initiative to show concern when my friend has problems.
❏	❏	18.	Seek my friend's counsel when I'm faced with a difficult decision or problem.
❏	❏	19.	Willingly inconvenience myself to help my friend.
❏	❏	20.	Respect my friend's right to privacy.

Chapter Three
The Right Foundation

Concept: We should be intentional in nurturing
our own spiritual lives – not only to be more effective
in sharing our faith but also to be more fruitful in
our own discipleship.

"You're just like the scribes and Pharisees, the hypocrites,
who made Jesus so angry. 'You cross land and sea to make a
single convert, and you make the new convert twice as much a
child of hell as yourselves.' Look it up in your Bible – the twenty-
third chapter of Matthew." She shook her finger at the young
man who stood in her front hallway; I was extremely thankful
not to be on the receiving end of her indignation. "Now get out
of here, and don't come back. The Lord has made me painfully
aware of my sins, and I don't need you to point them out. I also
don't need you to quote Scripture. You took the verses out of
context and just dumped on me. You'd better deepen your own
faith if you want to go around talking about it with others."

The woman was in her early thirties and had recently been
divorced. She was working sixty hours a week and raising three
children. In her search for a church home, she had visited both
the church that I pastored and the church of the overly zealous
pastor she had ordered out of the house. I had inadvertently
arrived there just a few minutes after him.

The eager cleric had not gotten off to a great start with her,
as he initially railed against the sin of divorce, suggesting that
her soul needed to be saved. He did not know that she had been
in an abusive relationship, divorcing her husband only after a
second hospitalization resulting from his brutal attacks. She
was also the daughter of missionary parents and had enormous
knowledge of the Bible.

We obviously shouldn't start to push our own ideas before we really understand another person's situation. The incident just described could have been used as an opening illustration for the chapter on listening! It also shows, however, the importance of continually working at our own spiritual growth. Had the other pastor been a little more mature in his own faith, he would not have felt such great need to inflict it on the woman before understanding the circumstances of her life.

We don't need extensive knowledge of the Bible or of doctrine in order to talk about our faith with other people. We do, however, need to be honest about our own doubts and misgivings and open about our failures. If we aren't serious about being transparent with our own faith, we are not likely to help others grow.

Joyce Neville in *How to Share Your Faith without Being Offensive* says: "Every Christian has a sacred story uniquely his own, even if he has not thought of it in those terms. This sacred story is comprised of many sacred chapters, some short, some long, some about happy experiences, some about sad ones. As Christians, our life story is a book written by God, a book to be shared as well as lived" [p. 30]. The more in touch we are with our own story, the more comfortable we will be sharing it with others.

A Spiritual Inventory

The goal of evangelism is to bring others into a growing, dynamic, life-changing relationship with God and the Christian community. We aren't likely to convince others of the life-changing power of God unless we are experiencing it in our own lives. We aren't likely to convince others of the importance of Bible study and prayer unless we practice those disciplines ourselves. What we model may be more important than what we say. The saying that "faith is more caught than taught" is true. Do you and I have an exciting, contagious faith? How do we go about continuing to grow in our own spirituality? An honest spiritual inventory or assessment can help in our own faith journey. Some questions to consider:

Do I have a healthy relationship with Jesus Christ and the Christian community? Do I have a healthy balance between recognizing that I can't earn my salvation and understanding that the gifts and skills given by God are to be used in the building of God's kingdom? Is my relationship with the church one-sided? Do I do a lot of giving but fail to allow others to minister to me?

Do I have a growing faith? Do I feel stuck in a rut with my faith? Has it become boring and routine? Have I grown spiritually in the last six months? Am I aware of how God is currently working with me to help my faith grow? What role, if any, does the church play in my spiritual development?

Do I have a dynamic faith? Is there power in my faith, or do I feel weak? Does my faith empower me for daily living? When I worship, pray, or read the Bible, does it feel like I am being renewed or just going through the motions? When I attend church, do I feel revitalized or drained?

Do I have a life-changing faith? Is my faith apparent in the way I live my life? Am I merely a Christian, or am I also a disciple? Is Jesus only my Savior, or is he also my Lord? Before making life-changing decisions, do I take a careful look at the teachings and example of Christ? Does the church help me understand what is distinctive about a Christian lifestyle and encourage me to live that way?

An honest spiritual inventory reveals deficiencies in all of us. Being a disciple of our Lord means being in a continuous process of growth. Some persons reflect on questions like those above and conclude that they have no business sharing faith with others. The status of our own spiritual health, however, does not disqualify us from Christian witness. All Christians, no matter what the condition of their faith development, are called to reach out through words and actions.

The purpose of a spiritual assessment is to identify both strengths and weaknesses. Where we have strengths, we need to continue building on them. Where we have weaknesses, we need to engage in spiritual exercises which will make us stronger. We also need to recognize the ways the church is part of our spiritual strength and can help us in our weakness.

Another crucial reason for growing in faith is to circumvent the common assumption that our own limited understanding is an adequate representation of the mighty creator God. One of the dangers of some doctrinal statements and some formula-like approaches to faith–sharing is the tendency to neatly package and market God – in the image of our own limited expectations. We need to approach God, not only in intimacy and friendship, but also in reverence and in awe:

To whom then will you compare me, or who is my equal? says the Holy One.
Isaiah 40:25

Therefore, since we are receiving a kingdom that cannot be shaken, let us give thanks, by which we offer to God an acceptable worship with reverence and awe; for indeed our God is a consuming fire.
Hebrews 12:28-29

In *The Trivialization of God*, Donald W. McCullough, the president of San Francisco Theological Seminary, suggests that we do not always know the power we invoke when we pray: "We prefer the illusion of a safer deity, and so we have pared God down to more manageable proportions" [p. 14]. Careful study of Scripture, regular prayer, and dialogue with people who are mature in their faith can help us grow closer to God recognizing the reality that we will **never** fully understand the Almighty!

McCullough also warns us concerning the well–intentioned exhortation to "invite Jesus into your heart." Obviously the image of Jesus coming into a person's heart is a strong one, playing a major, traditional role in evangelistic activity. McCullough asks: "But why on the basis of one verse, has an entire theology and language of 'personal acceptance' of Jesus swamped the far more pervasive apostolic call to confess 'Jesus is Lord?' The reason, I submit, is that it fits more comfortably with our American sensibilities. So long as *I* invite Jesus into *my* heart, I'm still in control of things and my personal freedom is in no way threatened" [p. 23].

A Lamp to Our Path

Psalm 119 is the longest psalm and a tribute to God's law. Several of these verses are both familiar and beautiful:

> *Oh, how I love your law! It is my meditation all day long. Your commandment makes me wiser than my enemies, for it is always with me.*
> **Psalm 119:97-98**
>
> *How sweet are your words to my taste, sweeter than honey to my mouth! Through your precepts I get understanding; therefore I hate every false way. Your word is a lamp to my feet and a light to my path.*
> **Psalm 119:103-105**

Consider the implications of four of the ten words used to designate God's law in Psalm 119:

- **Law** is more than a reference to the Torah or Pentateuch (the first five books of the Bible). It refers to all God has made known about his character and purpose.

- **Commandment** refers to more than observing the Decalogue (the Ten Commandments) and includes submitting to the will of a personal God who is in a covenant relationship with us.

- **Word** refers to something that is itself alive, coming out of a living person, conveying the power of the speaker, and changing the listener. John 1:1,14 tell us that Jesus is the *Word*.

- **Precepts** are detailed rules or standards for living that we are willing to follow and that constitute an alternative to making up our own rules.

All four words imply considerably more than an external observance of moral conduct. In fact, all ten words used for the law in Psalm 119 convey the reality that God has a purpose for our lives. When we strive to fulfill God's purpose for our lives, we are brought into greater harmony with the Almighty, with other people, and with ourselves.

Verses 97 and 98 urge us to meditate on God's law. Often our lives feel too busy, too hectic, and too stressed to stop, reflect, and pray. Without that reflection and meditation, however, we are likely to spend our lives on a treadmill, running and running, but getting nowhere. We are called to meditate on how God's law and God's will impact our lives: our strengths, our weaknesses, our actions, our thoughts, and our attitudes.

Verses 103 through 105 tell us that God's law guides us like a lamp to our feet and a light to our path. When we submit to God's will for our lives, virtually every aspect of our existence is affected. We may not always see far in advance the directions we should take, but we can be confident that we will have sufficient light available to make right decisions when they need to be made.

Struggle in the Garden

Matthew 26:36-42 vividly reminds us that we may often struggle with God's will for our lives. In the scene described by these verses, Jesus prays in the Garden of Gethsemane, preparing himself for crucifixion. Any person would shrink from the horror and cruelty of the cross, but Jesus is dealing with more than a painful and barbaric death. He is also dealing with the betrayal of one friend, the denial of another, and the desertion of the rest. He bears the sins of all people who have ever lived and who ever will live; and he still has mockery, beating, the cross, and death to endure.

Jesus understands the *cup* he must drink and is horrified by it, even if it is God's will. He says to his disciples: "I am deeply grieved, even to death" [v. 37]. Intense prayer is his only answer to the agony of his situation. The gospel of Luke tells us: "In his anguish he prayed more earnestly, and his sweat became like great drops of blood falling down on the ground" [verse 22:44].

God's will often brings great joy and meaning to our lives. There are other experiences, however, in which surrendering our lives to that will results in intense struggle. In our self-centeredness, we sometimes are unable to see any perspective except our own. We are also tempted to pervert God's will in order to bring it in line with our opinions, our prejudices, and our desires. For many of us, surrender to God's will is a daily, if not an hourly struggle. Intense prayer is absolutely necessary.

There is also tremendous loneliness in the struggle of Jesus to do God's will. Jesus takes three of his disciples – Peter, James and John – with him into the garden and asks them to watch with him while he prays. Jesus returns from prayer to find them asleep. In our spiritual walk, we always need the encouragement, support, and prayers of others. They can help us significantly on our spiritual journey, but they will sometimes let us down. In the final analysis, our walk with God cannot happen because of what someone else does or does not do to make it real and intimate. Each of us must develop his or her own unique relationship with Christ.

In his prayers in both verses 39 and 42, Jesus finds resolution to this lonely and agonizing struggle. The New Revised Standard Version uses the phrase *My Father* to describe the way Jesus addresses God in the midst of this situation. Mark's account of the time in Gethsemane maintains the Aramaic word *Abba*, which has a meaning perhaps most closely matched by our word *Daddy* [v. 14:36]. Jesus expresses the closest possible intimacy with God and dependence on God.

In both prayers, Jesus is very honest about what the human side would prefer: "If this is possible, let this cup pass from me" [26:39]. Jesus speaks openly in prayer about his doubts and reservations. A deepened spirituality does not come out of saying what we think God wants to hear. God is already aware of our deepest thoughts, anxieties, fears, hopes, and desires. *Spiritual maturity comes out of being open and honest with God about our real thoughts and feelings, even if we know they are contrary to God's will.* We can only properly deal with those realities of the inner life if we openly bring them to our conversations with God.

Finally, Jesus surrenders to God's will: "Yet not what I want, but what you want" [26:39]. The struggle has ended, Christ has accepted God's will, and humankind will be redeemed as a result.

Spiritual Disciplines

A word of caution! Using spiritual disciplines to nurture our faith can easily deteriorate into an external and works-oriented righteousness. We do not earn our salvation or increase our value as the children of God by practicing spiritual disciplines. Our salvation and our worth come to us through God's grace, not through our works. Spiritual disciplines are channels which help us be more open to God's presence and guidance.

There are some excellent books to guide us in spiritual growth. Two of the best are *Celebration of Discipline* by Richard Foster and *A Hunger for Healing* by Keith Miller. Both of these resources have study guides and videos available for use with small groups and classes. Here are some spiritual disciplines to consider as you seek to grow in your faith:

Prayer: Prayer is more than expressing our thanksgiving, confessing our sins, and seeking God's help for ourselves and others. Prayer needs to carry us to the very throne of God. As the writer of Hebrews says: "Let us then approach the throne of grace with confidence, so that we may receive mercy and find grace to help us in our time of need" [4:16, NIV]. Prayer needs to be a matter of living – an ongoing conversation with God. Prayer should include both talking to God and listening quietly for response. Prayer needs to be a discipline we practice individually and with other Christians.

Bible Study: Bible study helps us understand how the whole story of God's people fits together, the historical context of the biblical characters, and the kind of spiritual issues with which they were dealing. Bible study should ask: **So what?** We need to study Scripture seeking its relevance for our daily lives. Many good resources are available to help us with personal Bible study, but we should not neglect the discipline of group study. In groups we can compare our understanding of Scripture with that of other people in the body of Christ.

Worship: Worship is the central focus of the corporate life of the church. In worship, God's people come together into God's presence, acknowledge God's awesome nature, seek God's forgiveness, and offer themselves in God's service. But worship is an attitude more than it is a liturgy. As Paul wrote to the church at Rome: "I appeal to you therefore, brothers and sisters, by the mercies of God, to present your bodies as a living sacrifice, holy and acceptable to God, which is your spiritual worship" [Romans 12:1]. This attitude of complete dedication needs to pervade our corporate worship, our family worship, and our individual worship.

Personal devotions: All of us need to set aside daily time for Bible reading, inspirational reading, and prayer. Some find this best done when they first get up to set the tone for the day. Others prefer the lunch hour as a midday reminder of the source of who they are and all they do. Still others find an evening devotional time a perfect way to reflect back and end the day. The time of day often affects the nature of our devotional life. We are more likely to say "please" to God in the morning and "thank you" to God in the evening. For this reason, some people schedule more than one daily devotional time. There are many good resources for practicing daily devotions, including *The Upper Room* and *Our Daily Bread.*

Silence/Solitude: We all need times when we get away from the loud, distracting, and seductive voices around us. We all need to slow down and allow God to speak to us. Many of us feel under so much pressure that we become convinced all our waking moments should be filled with activity. And yet waking moments spent doing absolutely nothing can be the most productive we have in the day. We become too dependent on noise in our living environment – people talking, horns honking, dogs barking, and stereos or televisions blaring. We all need to find times when we shut everything and everyone off. We need to open ourselves to hear God and the silence of our own souls. Sometimes it is helpful to have a biblical passage or an inspirational reading to focus on during this time of silence and solitude. It is also helpful to build times of silence into our corporate worship, Sunday School classes, and Bible study groups.

Journaling: Writing in a personal journal is a wonderful way to reflect on one's life in a spiritual context. Journaling can be used to comment on Scripture or an inspirational reading. It can also be used to reflect on our thoughts, our feelings, our attitudes, our daily activities, and our relationships with God and with other people. Some people see journal writing as a daily letter to God.

Journal writing helps us in several ways. When we read journal entries of six months, twelve months, or a few years ago, we can better assess our spiritual growth. Journal writing also helps us recognize how well God responds to our prayers (though not always in the ways we expected). As we read earlier entries, we can identify concerns which have been resolved. This can motivate deeper thanksgiving and praise. Members of Bible study groups, small groups, and Sunday School classes who covenant to journal together can grow by sharing their findings with one another (though persons should never be put under pressure to share what they have written unless they wish to do so).

Spiritual guides and partners: Spiritual guides and partners are people with whom we can share openly, honestly, and confidentially the struggles and joys in our spiritual journeys. A **guide** could be someone who is greatly admired for his or her faith walk and who may be able to help another person on a spiritual journey. A **partner** may be someone who is not necessarily more experienced but with whom there is a mutual commitment to share support in the spiritual life. Twelve–step programs base much of their success on this kind of model – new members are urged to find a sponsor to help them along the way. Accountability can help keep us from drifting in unhealthy directions or deceiving ourselves by justifying sinful practices and lifestyles. Bible study groups, small groups, and Sunday School classes can encourage a deeper level of mutual accountability for those who are interested through the use of spiritual partners.

Service to others: Spiritual disciplines need to help us look both inwardly and outwardly. When we see the needs of those around us, we often experience God's call in their needs. When we respond to those needs, we learn about other people, ourselves, and the purpose for our lives in God's world. When we do acts of service, we become more Christ-like. We need to remember that Christ "did not come to be served, but to serve, and to give his life as a ransom for many" [Matthew 20:28, NIV].

Faith–Sharing: Sharing our faith with others is itself a spiritual discipline. When we share our faith, we put into words what being in relationship with God and God's people means for us. Public proclamation of our faith also serves to solidify it and give it strength. Faith–sharing needs to begin with other

Christians in a Bible study group, small group, Sunday School class, or friendship or family setting. This helps us learn to articulate our faith with those who are helping to nurture us in it. It's also good practice for sharing our faith with those outside the church. Future chapters will offer more specific suggestions.

There are other disciplines and exercises which help people grow in their faith, but space prohibits us from covering all of them – fuller elaboration on that topic would make this chapter a separate book! Most of us need to try several disciplines and then focus on the ones that are most helpful.

We also need to remember that spiritual disciplines help us look both inwardly and outwardly. If we are focusing on only one of those directions, we may need to try a different discipline for a time to broaden our focus. We need to use disciplines, not legalistically, but as channels for receiving God's transforming grace, a grace that affects our own lives, the lives of others, and the world of which we are a part.

Some Things to Try

1. The end of this chapter lists the spiritual disciplines which have been discussed and provides some blank space beside each one. For each discipline, write a few comments which share how comfortable you would feel practicing it and some possible ways you could begin practicing it. Place an **X** beside the two or three disciplines you would most like to start making part of your life, if you are not already doing so.

2. Study a book on the spiritual disciplines by yourself or with a class or group.

3. If you are not presently observing a daily devotional time, make plans to start. Identify:
   - A time.
   - A place.
   - Resources to use.
   - How to structure the time.

Commonly Used Spiritual Disciplines

*For each of the spiritual disciplines listed below, write a few comments which share how comfortable you would feel practicing it and some possible ways you could begin practicing it. Place an **X** beside the two or three disciplines you would most like to start making part of your life, if you are not already doing so.*

Prayer:

Bible study:

Worship:

Personal devotions:

Silence/solitude:

Journaling:

Spiritual guides or partners:

Service to others:

Faith–sharing:

Chapter Four
The Art of Listening

Concept: Cultivating the art of listening helps us understand others, enables us to show our concern, and provides the necessary foundation for us to speak meaningfully about our faith and the church.

Like many other aspects of the gospel, evangelism is a paradox. When we think about sharing our faith, we usually focus on talking:

- What words will we use?
- What examples will we share?
- How will we respond to questions?
- How comfortable will we feel as we talk?

In terms of building solid friendships, sharing our faith, and inviting people to church, however, listening is more important than talking. We can't speak to people meaningfully unless we do so in response to their needs, interests, and concerns. If we genuinely care about them and want to understand the dynamics at work in their lives, then we need to invest time in listening.

I once shared a personal struggle with a friend who was a clinical psychologist. As I kept talking about my problem, she kept interrupting with suggested solutions. I tried to ignore her well-intended advice and continued describing my problem. She nevertheless persisted in offering suggestions, clearly hoping to find a solution acceptable to me. In exasperation, I finally cried: "Please don't tell me what to do. I know what to do. I just need someone to listen and understand!

Without listening, we miss what Christ may be attempting to give us through our relationships with others. We also miss:

- Meeting people where they are.
- Being sensitive to their needs.
- Learning about opportunities to show our love and concern.
- Finding the natural bridges which can help us share the good news of Christ.

What the Bible Says About Listening

The Apostle James gives us important counsel about our relationships with others: "You must understand this, my beloved: let everyone be quick to listen, slow to speak" [**James 1:19**]. Human nature usually takes us in the opposite direction: we are often too quick to speak and too slow to listen. When we focus on speaking, we are focusing on ourselves – choosing the words we will use to express the ideas which we have. When we focus on listening, we are focusing on the person with whom we are in conversation – gaining knowledge of the factors at work in his or her life. It usually takes a conscious effort on our part to listen more than we speak.

Being quick to listen, as urged by James, means staying open to opportunities to hear the concerns of others. Unfortunately we sometimes experience some fairly self–centered thoughts when someone engages us in conversation:

- "If I keep listening to her, I'll never get finished with my work."

- "I sure get tired of hearing his litany of physical complaints."

- "If she would just be quiet and listen to me, I could solve her problem."

- "If he had paid any attention to me the last time we talked, I wouldn't be hearing this now."

All of those thoughts are inconsistent with the nonjudgmental attitude that Christ encourages in us.

Proverbs warns us of the danger of talking too much: "When words are many, transgression is not lacking, but the prudent are restrained in speech" **[Proverbs 10:19]**. Being a poor listener can actually be sinful! When we concentrate on sharing our own opinions and ideas rather than on understanding the needs of the other person, we may say things which will later appear foolish or even harmful.

A high school friend of mine once shared the following counsel: "If you're in doubt, don't say a word. It's better to keep your mouth shut and be thought a fool than to open it and remove all doubt!" In fact people who are restrained in their speech are often considered wise by others. Few people seriously criticize someone for being too quiet!

We have almost all found ourselves "running off at the mouth." Those are often the occasions when we say something which we later regret. The tongue is a powerful tool and can be used for both good and evil. Before speaking, we need to listen carefully to what the other person has to say. When we better understand the other person's point of view, we are more likely to choose words in response which will be helpful. The good judgment and common sense embodied in prudent speech are far easier to achieve when we have truly listened.

Becoming a Better Listener

In addition to the biblical case for listening carefully before speaking, there are several practical benefits to being a good listener:

- Listening helps the other person feel understood, which generally causes that person to feel less alone and isolated. Virtually all of us feel better about ourselves when another person has truly listened to us.

- Listening to another helps that person in self-understanding. When the person can put his or her private thoughts into words, there is usually an accompanying gain in perspective and insight. A good listener can act as a mirror for the person speaking.

- The person to whom we are listening will feel our concern and respect. By listening to the person, we are demonstrating that we accept that individual for who he or she is (even though we may not agree with everything the person says or does). In our silent attention to the words of that person, we convey the clear message that the individual is important to us.

Good listening goes beyond hearing words. Most of us have had the experience of standing in a grocery store check-out line with an agitated person behind us. The person's eyes look cross, the arms are folded across the chest, and there is obviously strain in the voice which says: "Don't worry about me. I'm in no hurry." We know instantly that the real message is not in the words and that this person would like us out of the way – SOON! We hear the real message in two ways:

- **First, we hear the real message in the tone of voice.** While the person's words may say he or she is calm and patient, the strained voice tells us of frustration and impatience.

- **Second, we recognize the real message in the person's body language.** We know the person is upset because of the arms folded across the chest and the agitated movement.

When we ask others a question such as "How are you doing today?", the stock answer is something like "Okay." The meaning of *okay* depends in large part on the tone of voice and the body language of the speaker.

Our body language toward those with whom we visit is an important component in good listening. We need to face the other person, lean forward showing our interest, and above all, maintain eye contact. Some have said that *the eyes are the windows of the soul.* That may not be literally true, but good eye contact certainly encourages deeper, more meaningful communication.

As we strive to become better listeners, we need to avoid some common habits:

1. Too often we only hear part of what a person says because we are busy mentally formulating our response. People may not get down to the nuts-and-bolts or the tough issues until near the end of the conversation. If we aren't listening carefully because we are preoccupied with our own words, we may miss an important key to understanding the person's situation.

2. We can too easily take the conversation off in our own direction. The person may refer to a word, idea, or experience that triggers one of our memories. Without realizing our rudeness, we may interrupt the person and start describing the memory.

3. We jump to conclusions too quickly. The person may share an experience similar to one we or others we know have had. Based on the previous experience, we may jump to conclusions about what the person needs. While situations may be similar, no two are exactly the same. Each person is a unique creation of God and may experience similar situations very differently from others.

4. We may also find ourselves judging the person if he or she talks about doing something of which we do not approve. Jesus warned us about the danger of judging others [Matthew 7:1-5, for example]. Judging is God's business, not ours. When we refuse to judge someone, we are communicating that person's inherent worth as a child of God. If the person is not a Christian, he or she may have a different value system from ours. No matter how strongly we may want that person to accept Christ and adopt the values we feel are consistent with the Christian faith, we have to respect the right of that person to hold a different world view.

5. We may try to tell people what they should feel. Feelings and emotions are a unique possession of each person. No one has the right to control the emotions of another, and in fact it's impossible to do so. Emotions are morally neutral – they are neither good nor bad. The moral issues surround what we say and do in response to the emotions we feel. Once a person has shared an emotion, especially one that is socially unacceptable or personally uncomfortable, he or she is often able to deal with it more clearly and rationally.

[In Matthew 5:21-28, a portion of the Sermon on the Mount, our Lord warns about the danger of harboring lust and anger. The fact that we experience such feelings is simply a part of the way God created us. The intent of these verses is not that the emotions themselves are wrong but rather that it is wrong to dwell on those emotions and related incidents to such an extent that we damage the spiritual life or relationships with others. If lust causes us to make another person become uncomfortable, we've moved from feelings to action. If anger causes us to curse another person, we've moved from feelings to action.]

6. We may be too quick to give advice. Giving advice implicitly puts us in a superior position to the person to whom we are listening. This one-upsmanship can quickly stifle deeper communication. When we tell people how to solve their problems, we are setting ourselves up for two potentially dangerous situations. If our advice is good, the person may become overly dependent on us instead of learning to solve his or her own problems. When our advice is less than perfect, we may be blamed when things don't work out the way the person had hoped.

Good listening is not a passive process, but a very active one. When we are good listeners, we need to invest a lot of time and energy; moreover, the hardest part about active listening often is hearing the unspoken emotions behind the words.

Active listening is reflective. As said before, it serves as a mirror back to the person to whom we are listening. In active listening, we first need to reflect or paraphrase back the content of what the person is saying: "What I hear you saying is that the demands of your job are becoming greater than the time and energy you have available." By reflecting back content, we do two things:

1. We demonstrate that we hear and understand the person. If what we reflect back is wrong, it can be corrected.

2. We help the speaker see his or her problem more objectively. The words come out of our mouths instead of that person's, and therefore it is easier for him or her to be objective about what is said.

After reflecting the content back, we then need to reflect back the feelings and emotions behind the words. Sometimes this may involve naming feelings of which the other person is totally unaware. For example: "I hear that you are very frustrated and angry that your boss is insensitive to what he is doing to you with all these demands."

People sometimes have strong feelings which come across in their tone of voice and body language even though not in the literal content of what is being said. Naming the emotions that we detect lets the other person test the validity of our observation. Having the emotion named, it often loses its overwhelming power. Thoughts and feelings are no longer jumbled together and confused. Then he or she can calmly deal with the feeling and the source of the feeling.

Sometimes in attempting to reflect back either content or emotions, we simply miss the boat. The person responds: "No, that's not what I'm saying at all!" When this happens, we need to avoid feeling guilty or feeling like we are bad listeners. Even the best of listeners occasionally misunderstands or misreads a person. When the person says we have reflected back inaccurately, that is a cue for us to ask more clarifying questions. We need to explore what he or she is saying until our perceptions of both content and emotions are accurate.

Active listening skills take practice. They cannot be mastered overnight. Active listening is like learning to ride a bicycle: the more we do it, the easier it becomes. Be patient with yourself!

Becoming a better listener not only improves one's ability to share the faith but also improves the quality of all relationships. This summary may help:

To Become a Better Listener . . .

- Focus on the other person's words.
- Hear the message conveyed in the tone of voice and in the body language of the other person.
- Show concern and interest in your own body language.
- Ask clarifying questions.
- Reflect back both content and emotions to the person who is speaking.

Some Things To Try

1. In your conversations during the next week, try to practice the skills of a good listener. Pay close attention to tone of voice and body language. Make a mental note whenever you use a bad listening habit. Work at reflecting back content and the emotions behind the content. Practice doing this with:

- A member of your family.
- A stranger you meet for the first time.
- A coworker or friend.

As you do this, take note of the impact that good listening skills had on your conversation. Did the person open up to you more? Did you understand the person better? Did you show the depth of your concern in the care with which you listened? How did you feel about yourself by relating to the person as a good listener?

2. If you have opportunity in a group, practice the rumor game with a slightly different twist. Have five people step out of the room. Explain to those who remain in the room what you are going to do. Then call the first person back into the room and describe the following incident to him or her:

> *I came out of the video store at the corner of Seventh and Elm Streets with two videos I had rented. An older woman in a gray sedan was backing out of the grocery store across the street. Just then a four-wheel drive pick-up came zooming down Seventh Street from the north; it was driven by a young man about twenty years old with blond hair. The left front of his pick-up hit the right rear of the woman's old sedan causing it to spin around two-and-a-half times. The young man in the four-wheel drive seemed okay, but the older woman was unconscious, sitting behind her steering wheel with cuts on her face and bruises on her arms. I went to a phone in the grocery store to call an ambulance.*

Invite the second person to return to the room, and ask the first person to relate the story as he or she remembers it. Then ask the third person to return to the room, and have the second person share the story. The third person should then tell the story to the fourth person, who will share it in turn with the fifth person. The fifth person will repeat the story to the entire group.

This is a great social game which will lead to lots of good-natured laughter. After the laughter subsides, visit together about why remembering the story was so difficult. How much could memory of the story have been improved if the listeners had asked clarifying questions?

3. Using the questionnaire at the end of this chapter titled "DOs and DON'Ts for Active Listeners," take a personal inventory to determine the quality of your listening skills. Determine two or three characteristics of a good active listener which you need to cultivate. Plan ways you can grow in these listening skills.

DOs and DON'Ts for Active Listeners

Read over the following characteristics of an active listener. Rate yourself on each skill using these symbols:

    A =   *Already skilled at this*
    N =   *Need practice at this*
    NS =   *New skill that I have never learned or practiced before*

A N NS 1. DON'T jump to conclusions about what the person is feeling or thinking.

A N NS 2. DON'T be judgmental or assign blame.

A N NS 3. DON'T interrupt. Let the person finish what he or she is saying.

A N NS 4. DON'T miss hearing what the person is saying because you are mentally busy thinking of how you should respond.

A N NS 5. DON'T give into the temptation to give advice or tell the person what he or she ought to do or feel.

A N NS 6. DO encourage the person to tell you more, both about the issue you are discussing and about himself or herself.

A N NS 7. DO pay attention to body language. It can tell you a lot about how the person is feeling (nervous, guarded, angry, etc.).

A N NS 8. DO maintain eye contact with the person as you listen. This demonstrates that you care and helps you better understand the person's feelings.

A N NS 9. DO listen for the person's tone of voice. The words may say one thing while the tone tells you what is really being felt.

A N NS 10. DO keep an attitude of prayer as you listen, so you can be aware of God's concern for the person who is speaking and for yourself.

Chapter Five
Moving Conversation
to Deeper Levels

Concept: We need to develop comfort in moving conversations to deeper levels, showing a willingness to talk about what's most important in life.

Several years ago, my wife and I attended an inspirational movie with two other couples. We stopped at a restaurant on the way home for pie, coffee, and conversation. Because I had been deeply touched by the movie, I asked the others how the film had spoken to their faith experience. Rather than eliciting the meaningful dialogue I had anticipated, my question produced an awkward silence. As soon as someone changed the subject to a more superficial topic, discussion picked up again.

Having faith in Christ does not automatically make it easy for us to share our observations and feelings about the big questions and significant issues of life. When we share at that level, we become vulnerable and expose our true selves to possible criticism and rejection. People are far more comfortable discussing family activities, work issues, sports, and other interests than topics which are rooted in the very heart of their being. Discussing matters of the heart does require tremendous trust and emotional investment on everyone's part, but never venturing into these deeper subjects leaves our relationships shallow and makes us feel alone and isolated. We both crave and fear intimate communication. Far too often, the victory is given to fear.

One of the main reasons that evangelism and personal faith–sharing feel so difficult is that sharing at that level can leave us vulnerable and exposed. Many of us are tempted to excuse ourselves from such conversations by simply "living our faith" rather than actually talking about it. While we certainly need to reflect our faith in our actions, the actions alone will not necessarily bring others closer to God. People will often fail to understand the motivations behind our actions unless we verbally explain.

Like us, the person with whom we are seeking to talk about our faith may appear to prefer keeping the dialogue at a relatively superficial, safe level. What happened to me during the pie and coffee stop after the movie isn't unusual. I nevertheless believe that all of us carry within a desire for more intimate communication and relationship. People look for signs which identify individuals with whom real life issues can be shared. We need to recognize that desire in others, watch for signs of openness, and learn how to move conversations to more meaningful levels.

The Woman at the Well

Jesus was a master of taking conversations to matters of the heart. **John 4:7-26** describes his encounter with a Samaritan woman beside Jacob's well at the city of Sychar. The conversation started simply enough with Jesus asking her to draw him a drink of water from the well. Before their meeting ended, however, she had revealed the deepest problems in her life, exposed her spiritual hunger, and accepted Jesus as the Messiah. How did Jesus accomplish this?

Our Lord was willing to cross social barriers. There were three reasons why a respectable Jewish man would never have participated in the exchange at the well:

- First, she was a woman. Jewish men were not in the habit of engaging women in conversation in public places.

- Second, she was a Samaritan. No respectable Jew would have anything to do with a person from Samaria.

- Third, we later learn that the woman was a sinner.

A Jewish man would not associate publicly with a
known sinner because it could tarnish his image.

Jesus, however, was willing to take the risks and cross all three
barriers. He began by asking the woman for a drink of water.

Entering into matters of the heart requires that we take risks
and cross barriers. Whether encountering a stranger or a potentially difficult topic for conversation, many of us want to hold
back and wait on the other person to initiate the dialogue. If the
other person is willing to talk, our role as a listener is
appropriate; but if the other person does not feel comfortable
beginning a discussion or moving the visit to a more intimate
level, then the caring response on our part is to move ahead by
sharing our own observations or, more often, by asking the right
questions.

We may need to cross some other barriers as we seek to reach
out to those outside the church. We often need to walk around
or move through social, economic, and ethnic barriers –
becoming friends with people of different races, nationalities, or
cultures. For some of us, another person's physical handicap or
simply unkempt appearance may stand as a barrier which needs
to be crossed.

**The moral barrier can be one of the most difficult to
overcome.** Christ confronted that barrier as he continued his
visit with the woman at the well. We may have to push ourselves to engage in meaningful conversations with persons
whose language, behavior, or reputation is offensive to us. Our
thoughts can easily become consumed with anxiety over how
other people will perceive us if we spend time with a particular
person. Yet our Lord consistently responded to individuals
without regard for what others would think. When the respectable, righteous people of Jesus' day sought to find fault with
him, they asked his disciples: "Why does your teacher eat with
tax collectors and sinners?" [Matthew 9:11, NIV].

The woman at the well immediately sensed Jesus' willingness
to talk with her, but this caused her to question his intentions.
Instead of becoming defensive about his motives, Jesus
immediately took the conversation to an intimate level. He talked about "the gift of God" and "living water."

The woman appeared put off by Jesus' attempt at a more serious conversation about spiritual matters. First, she criticized Jesus for having nothing with which to draw water. Then she questioned whether Jesus was greater than the ancestor Jacob who dug the well from which her townspeople drank.

Jesus was not deterred by side issues or defensive about aspersions on his character. He pointed out that even Jacob's well gave people only temporary relief from their thirst, while his *living water* would give them eternal life. The woman appeared too caught up in everyday issues to deal with spiritual concerns. She was tired of going to the well for water and wanted the living water to spare her from this daily task. She asked Jesus to give her living water, but her request reflected a spiritual hunger as well as a desire for relief from a chore. People will often disguise a spiritual need with an everyday request like: "Do you have time to do lunch this week?"

Then Jesus took the conversation to the heart of the matter – the problems with her family situation. How did Jesus know she had such difficulties? Most Jewish women came for water early, during the cool of the morning; but this woman came by herself in the heat of the noon-hour. Even without divine insight into her soul, Jesus could have wondered if there was behavior in her life that made her an outcast from the other women of the village. When we talk to people, do we pick up on words, phrases, and behaviors which might hint at the real problems with which a person is struggling? Jesus asked about her family life, not in a judgmental or condemning way, but out of sincere concern for her.

Recognizing Jesus' sensitivity to her problems, she confessed she had no husband. Parts of this dialogue may be missing because of its length, but Jesus either heard enough to know or learned from divine insight that she had been married five times and was now living with someone who was not her husband.

The woman brought up the different religious practices of Jews and Samaritans, who claimed to worship the same God. Jesus sidestepped this diversion and talked about the spirit and truth needed in meaningful worship. Faith–sharing conversations can be side-tracked into debate over denominational and ritualistic differences. We need to remember that personal spiritual needs are more pressing than controversial ecclesiastical debates.

Convinced that Jesus cared about her spiritual needs, the woman expressed her personal longing for the Messiah to come. In his coming, she hoped that she might find forgiveness for her sins and help with other problems. Because of the sincerity of her spiritual desire, Jesus revealed his identity and the reality that he could answer her deepest spiritual needs. Through probing questions, sensitivity, and deeper sharing, Jesus moved a casual visit about a drink of water into one in which a spiritually hungry woman recognized and accepted him as the Messiah.

Levels of Communication

Before we discuss communication skills that allow for more intimate conversations, consider the five levels of communication which can occur:

Exchanging Greetings. This level of social communication acknowledges another person but does not normally involve exchanging information. We find this level in simple sentences and questions such as: "Good morning!" or "How are you today?" or "How do you like this weather?" While this level of communication may be viewed by some as superficial, we certainly need to socially acknowledge others before we can take conversations further.

Exchanging Facts and Information. In this level of conversation, we learn more about the other person; and that person learns more about us. We find out about family, work, home towns, hobbies, and other interests. As a pastor, I have found this period of information gathering is crucial. When I ask a person about different aspects of his or her life at this level, that individual almost immediately responds with greater openness because of my evident interest. If we are listening sensitively, we may find that the other person revealed more than he or she realized.

Exchanging Opinions and Ideas. Once we become more familiar with a person, we begin sharing opinions and ideas about various topics including sports, politics, social issues, and even religion. Unfortunately, too many Christians believe that this is as deep as one needs to go to have a successful evangelistic encounter. We falsely believe that, if another person apparently shares our opinions about Jesus Christ, he or she is consequently a Christian like us. True Christianity is not based on opinions about Christ, but on a life-changing relationship with Christ. Many people acknowledge the basic theological and biblical truths associated with the Christian faith but make no effort to change their lives and bring them under Christ's Lordship. It takes more than right theology to make a Christian. And it takes more than a conversation at an opinion level to reveal the depths of how the Christian faith can change our lives.

Exchanging Feelings and Needs. At this level of communication, we become more vulnerable and open with one another, and the basis for real friendship and intimacy forms. Some feelings of safety and trust must have been established in the relationship if this level of conversation takes place, and those feelings need to be nurtured. We only become vulnerable with people when we trust them not to judge us but to accept us. Sharing feelings with someone we trust is both difficult and rewarding. We must feel close to others to share feelings like these:

- I'm frustrated with . . . .

- I'm angry at . . . .

- I feel hurt when . . . .

- I love you because. . . .

Like feelings, personal needs are only expressed with those persons who have proven themselves sensitive and responsive. Needs are not the same as wants and have to do with the basic physical, emotional, social, and spiritual necessities of the abundant life Jesus promised. We share more about needs in the sixth chapter.

Peak Communication. This level of communication is difficult to describe. It happens when two people establish an exceptional level of intimacy by their willingness to share with each other. Commitment and life-transforming experiences happen at this level. Empathy, which is another quality we will discuss in the sixth chapter, is essential in order for peak communication to occur. In peak communication:

- People may share things they have never said to another person.

- People may open up about their deepest fears and insecurities.

- People may verbalize the depths of their loneliness, frustration, or pain.

- People can experience love which transforms their lives.

- People are exceptionally open to each other and are communicating clearly in words, tone of voice, and body language.

- People may talk with complete openness about the big questions and issues such as: the meaning of life, what happens at the time of death, the nature of evil, why people suffer, and how God is at work in our lives.

- People talk freely and openly about their religious faith or lack of faith and its impact on their lives.

Faith–sharing is at its best during such peak communication.

Moving Conversation to Deeper Levels

The question for us now becomes: what kind of good listening skills do we need to develop in order to take conversations to deeper levels? Two communication skills which can be utilized are: (1) asking open-ended questions, and (2) asking deeper questions.

Open-ended questions invite comment and conversation. In contrast, closed-ended questions can be answered with a "yes" or "no," one word, or a short phrase. For example, closed-ended questions we might ask a new neighbor are: "Where did you live before?" "When did you move in?" and "How big is your family?"

Those questions serve a purpose in finding out more about another person during the initial stages of contact, but they do not take the conversation to a deeper level. Rephrasing those questions to make them open-ended, we might ask: "What was the town you used to live in like?" "What are some of your first impressions of our town?" and "Tell me more about your family." Open-ended questions invite sharing:

- What does it feel like to . . . ?

- Tell me more about . . . ?

- What do you think about . . . ?

- How did you learn to do . . . ?

- How would you describe . . . ?

In faith sharing, open-ended questions are essential to the possibility of peak communication. A commonly misused closed-ended question in faith–sharing is: "Are you saved?" With this question, responses are limited to a few words and phrases like "Yes," "No," "I don't know" and "What business is that of yours?" A more open-ended approach is needed to share meaningfully about a topic as personal and as crucial as salvation. For example, a discussion on salvation might begin: "I hear a lot of people talk about being saved. What do you think it means to be saved? What do you think we need to be saved from?" When we ask those kinds of questions, we may hear responses with which we disagree or which cause us to be upset; but that's precisely because the exchange is honest and open. If we can listen without judging or rejecting the other person, we will come to the opportunity to share our faith when that individual is ready to listen. We may learn things which will make it easier and more natural to share our faith in response to what the other person has experienced in life.

In addition to asking open-ended questions, we also want to ask questions which intentionally move the conversation to deeper levels. For example, we may be talking with a person about his or her interest in music, whether that means Bach, the Beatles, Michael Jackson, Metallica, Buddy Holly, Liz Phair, or Amy Grant. Such exchanges can easily focus on comparing and contrasting likes and dislikes. We might take the conversation further by asking something like this: "What do you think it is about the human spirit that attracts us to music? What needs does music fill? Does music speak to the soul?" Again, we may hear responses with which we disagree or which cause us to feel uncomfortable; but our purpose is not to judge the other person but rather to grow in our mutual understanding. When that happens, the other person will have greater openness to what we may want to say about our views on the place of music in life, in the church, or in personal faith.

Asking deeper questions can be used as a listening skill with almost any topic of conversation, but asking these questions requires some sensitivity and creative thinking. Above all, we need to be caring and genuinely interested in hearing the other person's opinions and feelings about these issues. This is not a ploy to manipulate the discussion, but a sincere way to build a more intimate and trust-filled friendship.

Such questions are best raised in one-to-one communication rather than in a group setting. The exception would be if there is an incredible amount of openness and trust in the group. Usually group settings for such discussions only invite debate, and one or two people dominate the conversation. In a one-to-one exchange, well-chosen questions invite intimacy and sharing of the feelings, needs, and beliefs which are often unspoken.

The conversation over pie and coffee, which was shared at the beginning of this chapter, illustrates the reality that not every discussion can be moved to a higher level of communication. If people display resistance or unwillingness to share at a more intimate level, we need to let it go. People will only let us pursue the deeper levels of communication when sufficient trust is built and when the setting feels right. Building trust in any relationship takes time.

> *Remember: these are listening skills which must be learned. Becoming comfortable asking open-ended and deeper questions take time. Be patient with yourself in the learning process.*

Some Things To Try

1. This week, take the risk of approaching a stranger at work or in a community setting. Ask that person about his or her job, family, place of birth, hobbies, and interests. As the conversation progresses, notice what happens to each of you: Does the other person seem more comfortable and relaxed talking with you? Do you feel more comfortable and relaxed talking with that person? As you learn more about the other person, make a mental note of any common interest which might be grounds for future conversations or further social contact.

2. The end of this chapter has an exercise on "Asking Open-Ended Questions." Take the closed-ended questions listed in the left column and rewrite them as open-ended questions in the right column.

3. The end of the chapter also has an exercise on "Asking Deeper Questions." Using the topics listed in the left hand column, write down questions in the right hand column that may take the conversation to a more intimate level.

4. Practice your skill at asking such questions in your interactions with people in your home, place of employment, community settings, and the church. The refinement of your skill will improve the quality of your relationships with others, even if these are not persons with whom you eventually share your faith.

Asking Open-Ended Questions

The column on the left lists some closed-ended questions. In the right column, rewrite the questions to make them open-ended. Remember: closed-ended questions can be answered in one or two words. Open-ended questions invite the person to share more with you. An example has been provided.

Closed-ended Questions	Open-ended Questions
How big is your family?	Tell me about your family.
How many children do you have?	
Where do your children live?	
Does your family like to travel?	
What do you do for a living?	
Do you like your job?	
When did you move here?	
Were you born & raised near here?	
Are your parents living?	
Do you know my friend Joe?	
Do you go to church?	
Are you "saved?"	
Do you believe in God?	
(List your own examples below)	

Asking Deeper Questions

The left column lists several topics you might discuss with other people. In the right column, write some deeper questions you could ask about these topics, as in the example beside "Sports."

Topics I discuss	Deeper questions I could ask:
Sports	Why do you think winning is so important? How do you feel when your team loses? Why is it so important to you to do your very best?
Family & Children	
Hobbies & Travel	
Job & Career	
Possessions (Clothes, VCRs,....)	
Education	
Church & Religion	

Chapter Six
Showing Concern

> **Concept:** Words and actions of genuine love and
> concern in response to the needs of people can be
> a powerful witness to our faith and should often
> precede efforts to communicate our faith verbally.

Michael moved to Houston because of an employment offer
from a software development firm located there. His first two
months in town were filled with eighty-hour weeks as he sought
to better understand how things were done in the firm and as he
endeavored to better understand the other people on the eight-
member development team to which he had been assigned. He
was replacing a person who had been with the team for three
years, and it was obvious that the other team members wondered whether or not Michael could cut it in terms of the sophisti-
cated work which was expected. He continually felt "on trial," in
spite of the superficially good-natured bantering that came from
the others.

At the start of his third month in Houston, Michael decided
to move out of the temporary housing in which he had been
living and to purchase a condominium in a part of town where
many other people his age lived. The paperwork was quickly
processed, and by the end of the month, he (and the mortgage
company) owned the condo.

In the middle of his fourth month, Aaron, who was called
the token Republican on the team because of his conservative
political positions on most issues and his daily reading of *The
Wall Street Journal*, came to work with news that got the
attention of everyone else – their relatively small company of 200

employees had been purchased by a huge software company in Seattle. *The Wall Street Journal* had been filled with information about stock prices, and Aaron was especially pleased because, as one of the long-time employees of the company, he had received a great deal of stock as part of his compensation.

Later that day an official announcement from the firm came saying that there would be a move of the entire operation to Seattle and that people would be getting individual word on their role in the coming reorganization. Later that afternoon, the personnel director gave Michael the bad news. Seventy-five jobs were going to be eliminated; and with his limited tenure, he would be one of those. Since he had been there such a short time, he only qualified for two months of severance pay, which the personnel director thought was pretty generous under the circumstances.

But it didn't feel generous to Michael who was now the owner of a condominium which had depleted his savings and stuck him with a twenty-year mortgage. Houston was a major urban area, but there was no other company offering opportunities like those for which he thought he had moved there. His best job options were going to be on the east coast or the west coast. He knew virtually no one in the city except the people on his team (none of whom had drawn close to him), the loan officer at the mortgage company, and the real estate agent.

Michael's depression grew over the next few weeks. He had never felt so alone or isolated. He spent his days looking at want ads, making appointments, going for interviews, and talking by phone with possible connections in other cities. Nothing looked promising. There were plenty of jobs outside his field, but none of those paid enough to meet his needs.

Not feeling comfortable alone in his condominium at night, he started spending his evenings driving all around Houston, occasionally stopping at a bar for a drink. He knew that he was developing a drinking problem, but he really didn't care. His only anxiety was the fear that he might have an automobile accident and hurt someone else.

As he drove around, he kept noticing that the city seemed filled with churches, some of them huge but some of them very small. He remembered being active in a small church while growing up in the Midwest and recalled the sense of security he had felt in Sunday school during his elementary school years and in junior high. He had stopped attending during high school. Michael had never stopped believing in God, or at least he didn't think he had. The truth, he supposed, was that he simply didn't think much about God.

But now Michael was thinking a great deal more about God than he had for many years. He felt deserted by God, and he also felt pulled toward God. He finally decided to go into one of those churches on Sunday morning, hoping for an encounter with God or at least hoping for some kind of contact with another human being who would care what was happening in his life.

Caring

The word "caring," like the word "friendship," has been used so much that in some respects it has lost meaning:

- "We care about you at St. Paul's hospital."

- "Fidelity Mutual cares about you and your family."

- "John Henry Ford: The Car Dealer Who Cares."

- "United Henry County Fund Drive – Together We Care"

There may well be truth in all four of the above statements. The respective organizations and causes may truly seek to create an atmosphere in which people feel they are cared for or that they are part of extending care to others. But the car dealer who cares and the joint caring envisioned by a county fund drive for social service agencies are not quite the same thing. And neither the opportunity to be "cared for" as a customer by the automobile dealer nor the opportunity to be part of "caring for" the less fortunate through the fund drive provides the kind of caring which Michael needed.

Then some other questions arise about Michael's situation. If one or more of the members of his team at work were Christians, would they in fact have shown him a level of care greater than that which he experienced? When he went to church, would he find an encounter with God and the genuine concern of other people? For that matter, people like Michael who come to church are often very reluctant to acknow-ledge that they do have problems or needs. If an atmosphere isn't created in which those needs can be shared comfortably, they may go unrecognized.

We all experience a certain amount of tension over our desire to be cared for and our desire for independence. That is part of the dilemma for a person like Michael who needs help but also wants to appear successful and in control. There are some situations in which we have a *desire* to be cared for by someone else; there are other situations in which being cared for moves from being a desire to being a *need.*

Michael in fact did go to a large church and did, during his second week of attendance, find his way into a Sunday school class of other persons his age. He did not, however, feel comfortable telling people the extent of his problems. He had just met these people, and he certainly didn't want to give the impression of being a weak person or of coming to church in an effort to get some kind of networking help or a handout. Because of that, several weeks passed before Michael actually told a couple of people after Sunday school class about his problems. The responses he received made him feel better for the rest of that day, but the next day he wondered why he had bothered confiding. The people had said to him:

> "Well, I want you to know that we care about you
> during this time of hardship and that we sure want
> to do anything we can to be of help. Just let us know."

> "I do care about you, and you are in my prayers."

What could they do to be of help? Find him a job? Point him to someone they know in a large company who can help him get past the reception desk? You don't ask people you've just met for that kind of help. For that matter, he had no idea if either person had any possibility of offering that level of assistance. There was no concrete benefit to Michael, and he found himself feeling awkward the next week as the woman who had said she would pray for him shared the concern aloud with the class and asked everyone to pray.

The next week, however, Michael, who was now living on checks written against the credit lines of his Visa and Master Card accounts, received a phone call which was a pleasant surprise. Connie, who had been part of his team at the software company, called to say that she had been thinking about him. Connie said, apparently feeling a little awkward doing so, that she had the habit of praying at the start of each day for people she knew. His name had kept coming into her mind, and she had begun to feel increasingly troubled about his situation.

"We weren't exactly warm and welcoming when you came to work," she said. "The truth is that we were still missing too much the person you replaced, and we weren't fair to you. I especially regret that now because of what happened to you. My husband Bob and I decided not to move to Seattle; but losing my job right now doesn't hurt us because his job is good and I own so much stock in the company. But we had a similar experience to what you're going through. He came here for a job with an oil company that downsized the fifth month we were in Houston. We'd decided to start a family when we moved here, and I was pregnant; but I ended up taking the job at the software company because we were so desperate for money. Bob was a house-husband for a long time before a job opening came that worked for him at the same time that we found day care that was good for our first child."

She invited Michael to have dinner with them. After dinner, she and her husband talked with him about some contacts that could be beneficial. Michael had a wonderful time visiting with them and was delighted by their two children. Bob and Connie kept checking on leads for him, made phone calls on his behalf, and had him in their home on numerous occasions. He never told them the extent to which those meals not only strengthened his emotional life but also helped him squeak by financially, though he had a feeling they knew.

He also started going to church with them, to another congregation of the same denomination he had been attending but on almost the opposite side of the city. He found temporary employment in his field through one of Connie's contacts, and he also found a warm and welcoming atmosphere in Connie and Bob's congregation. Nine months later he moved to the east coast to accept a job arranged through an old college friend, but he left Houston refreshed and renewed in his spiritual life and in his comfort with others. Three years later, he and the woman he married would name their first child Connie and invite Bob and Connie to become the child's godparents.

Note in this situation that the people in the first church he attended in Houston weren't necessarily "bad" in how they responded to him. In many respects, their response was very positive. They were seeking to be affirming, and the woman who asked the whole class to pray no doubt assumed that Michael would not mind and probably anticipated that he would appreciate their concern.

Connie certainly had failed to be the kind of caring, Christian presence for Michael in the workplace that she wished she had been. Connie, however, did anticipate some of what he must be going through and reached out in a very direct way that made a tremendous difference in Michael's life.

The invitation to Michael to attend church with them came so naturally that it was almost an afterthought. It happened at the end of a late night discussion in which the three of them had talked about what sometimes felt like a struggle to grow closer to God and to understand how God works in their lives. Michael had wondered aloud whether or not the prayers of the class in the other church had been part of what caused Connie to think about him in her own prayer life. Connie agreed that was likely the case, but Bob felt God rarely worked in that direct a fashion. Michael had expressed his own doubts about God and also acknowledged his own growing faith. Christ was becoming real for him in the presence of these caring people.

Sympathy – Empathy

Listening to others is an important part of friendship and of creating a climate in which sharing the faith and inviting others to church become natural and appropriate responses. When listening reveals that other people have significant problems in their lives, we need to respond to them with concern. We may not always be able to show concern at the level that Connie and Bob did, with temporary employment actually being the result of that concern; but we can always find meaningful ways to respond.

Modern psychology and English language usage have drawn a distinction between sympathy and empathy. *Sympathy* is an act of compassion, often involving an expression or feeling of sorrow for the pain, suffering, or difficulty of another person. *Empathy* involves more actual identification with another person's situation and feelings.

Both sympathy and empathy can be valid responses to the needs of others, but sympathy alone doesn't generate the bonding with another person that comes with true empathy. Empathizing with another doesn't necessarily mean agreeing with that person's response to the situation, but it does mean strongly identifying with it and understanding it. Paul understood empathy well when he wrote to the Romans:

> *Rejoice with those who rejoice, weep with those*
> *who weep. Live in harmony with one another;*
> *do not be haughty, but associate with the lowly;*
> *do not claim to be wiser than you are. Do not repay*
> *anyone evil with evil, but take thought what is*
> *noble in the sight of all. If it is possible, so far*
> *as it depends on you, live peaceably with all.*
> **Romans 12:15-18**

The people who visited with Michael at the first church certainly showed him sympathy by their responses. Connie, however, displayed empathy, because she truly identified with being Michael being unemployed in an unfamiliar city. In a sense she was feeling what Michael was feeling, though obviously not at exactly the same immediate intensity. While the fact that she had experienced such a similar situation in the past was a great help to her in that process, it isn't necessary to have precisely the same experiences as another person in order to display empathy.

Empathy in a sense means feeling and showing happiness when our friends are happy and feeling and showing sadness when our friends are sad. This doesn't mean that we let our friends control our emotions all the time. What it does mean is that we seek to become so aware of what our friends experience that we pick up on their feelings and experience them ourselves. We love our friends enough that, when they go through something, it affects us too. When a friend sees that we are deeply affected by his or her needs, our concern will be felt and understood.

Paul also reminds us in the passage from Romans that we don't need to claim to be wiser than we are or to have answers which we in fact don't have. We won't be able to solve all the problems our friends have, and that isn't expected of us. We are called to identify with and care for our friends, not necessarily to give advice or counsel in every situation. The process of caring can be summarized in three steps:

1. Hear not only the problem which is stated but also the need which lies behind the problem.

2. Come to truly understand the need.

3. Respond to the need in a way which is appropriate to the circumstances.

Understanding the Needs of Others

Various psychologists and other professionals have attempted to group human needs into categories to make it easier to understand them. Psychologist Abraham Maslow's system has five categories:

Physical needs are reasonably obvious. Every person needs food, water, fresh air, clothing, and shelter. Most of the people we encounter on a frequent basis will not have serious unmet needs in this category. Michael, however, was starting to experience problems in this area; and the meals provided to him were a significant help.

The need for security is often present in the worries and anxieties of the persons around us. We can be anxious about past mistakes, future well-being, what others think of us, and safety from harm from others. While a person like Michael who is unemployed obviously has high anxiety about such things, it isn't necessary to be in that situation to experience problems in terms of the need for security. For example, all of the following persons may be experiencing problems in terms of that need:

- The elderly person living in a changing neighborhood and feeling it is not safe to walk to the store after dark.

- The college student who isn't sure if there will be enough money available for the next year's tuition and fees.

- The person who has been to prison and in no way represents a present threat to others but is continually scared of rejection in the neighborhood, on the job, and perhaps even in church.

The need for love is as essential to well-being as the need for air, for water, or for food. People who feel lonely, isolated, or rejected are not able to function at their best and sometimes cannot function at all. Part of the difficulty for a person like Michael, stranded in Houston with significant problems and without close friends, comes in the absence of relationships with persons who will extend affection to him. Connie and Bob opened their homes and their hearts to him and extended the love of Christ when it made a difference. Think about the situations which cause people to miss the love that they need:

- Elderly persons who outlive significant numbers of their friends and end up living in nursing homes surrounded by strangers who did not know them during their prime.

- People with physical disabilities who often feel self-conscious and who may feel rejected by those who are uncomfortable around them.

- Persons in the armed forces who may be assigned across the world from their friends and families.

- Students who leave home for college and enter new learning, working, and living circumstances without the nearby support of family and of long-term friends.

The need for self-worth often surfaces in persons who are deeply depressed much of the time. Such persons have talents and abilities but are not always fully aware of them or have not had opportunities to use those skills and abilities in ways that would make a difference. Persons who have lost their jobs through corporate downsizing, who have been terminated from employment for other reasons, who have failed an educational program, or who have been through a divorce are all likely to experience extremely low self-worth.

Obviously there are persons who seem so full of themselves that they are described as arrogant, self-absorbed, or overbearing. While those labels may well be true, people who are overly focused on proclaiming their own worth, on examining their own lives perpetually, or on demonstrating their power and authority are usually people who deep within have very low self-worth. The objectionable outer characteristics are part of the mechanism by which they deal with the low self-worth.

For a Christian, of course, knowing that one is truly a child of God, created out of God's infinite love, is the best basis of all for positive self-worth. Even fully feeling the love of Christ and the affirmation of worth associated with that, however, one also needs to experience that affirmation from other people.

The need for self-actualization is highest level of need, in that this need manifests itself more when the other needs have been at least reasonably satisfied. Some Christians have come to understand this need as God-actualization, becoming all that God has intended.

This category may well apply to friends who are discussing their hopes, dreams, frustrations, and aspirations in relationship both to their careers and to their lives as a whole. This also may apply to persons who are probing deep questions about the meaning of life and why people suffer.

When people are frustrated at the level of basic needs such as physical well-being and security, they are not likely to focus strongly on the needs for love, for self-worth, or for self-actualization. In terms of helping people move closer to God, we need to remember that people who are blocked at the basic level are not likely to be receptive to discussions about higher level concerns. There are instances, of course, of people who are so fulfilled at the level of self-actualization that they have increased strength to deal with deprivation in terms of physical and security needs, but those persons are relatively few in number.

Our Lord shared this perspective on responding to the needs of others:

> *For I was hungry and you gave me food. I was thirsty and you gave me something to drink, I was a stranger and you welcomed me, I was naked and you gave me clothing, I was sick and you took care of me, I was in prison and you visited me. . . Truly I tell you, just as you did it to one of the least of those who are members of my family, you did it to me.*
> **Matthew 25:31-46**

When we respond to the needs of others, it is as though we are responding to the needs of our Lord. That alone should be sufficient motivation for us.

Other problems can arise when a person begins to confuse wants and needs. If a person's physical needs can only be met to his or her satisfaction by having a 3,000 square foot house, an imported luxury automobile, and a boat, then that person has seriously confused wants with needs. That generally means the individual's real unmet needs are not for physical things but for self-worth and love. The confusion of wants with needs can block a person from the ability to focus on higher needs like self-actualization.

Maslow's categories of need are perhaps the most helpful from a Christian viewpoint, but there are other systems. William Glasser, for example, speaks of:

1. The need to survive and reproduce.
2. The need to belong – to love, share, and cooperate with others.
3. The need for freedom.
4. The need for fun.

The need for fun may not seem equal in importance to the others listed, but consider how far people will go in the pursuit of pleasure and recreation. As Glasser says in his book *Control Theory*: "We will make drastic alterations in the way we live, even risk our lives, as we attempt to play to satisfy this need" [pp. 13-14]. While Glasser does not list religion as a basic need, he qualifies that by saying: "The bulk of the evidence is that for many, religion may be a basic need" [*Control Theory*, p. 17].

In his inspirational book *Man's Search for Meaning*, Viktor Frankl says that: "The striving to find a meaning in life is the primary motivational force in man" [p. 154]. That book grew out of Frankl's concentration camp experiences, and he speaks of the difference made in the lives of people who had found meaning and purpose even in the worst of circumstances:

> *We who lived in concentration camps can remember the men who walked through the huts comforting others, giving away their last piece of bread. They may have been few in number, but they offer sufficient proof that everything can be taken from a man but one thing: the last of the human freedoms – to choose one's attitude in any given set of circumstances, to choose one's own way.* [p. 104]

Choosing one's own way in the most difficult circumstances, when the needs of physical well-being and security are being continually threatened, only becomes possible when one has a clear sense of the meaning of life, or to use Maslow's terms, has achieved a very high degree of self-actualization. Frankl is also careful to point out that there is not a single "meaning in life" to which everyone ascribes but rather the meaning of life is for each person to discover in the process of his or her interaction with God, with other people, and within the self.

The hunger or thirst for meaning can also be seen as the hunger or thirst for God. We find these familiar words in Psalm 42:

> *As a deer longs for flowing streams,*
> *so my soul longs for you, O God.*
> *My soul thirsts for God, for the living God.*
> *When shall I come and behold the face of God?*
> **Psalm 42:1-2**

When we truly believe that a longing for God is deeply rooted within each person, then we are freed of the burden of feeling that we must immediately make some kind of verbal witness. That can be helpful under some circumstances; but generally speaking, we will be better carriers of the good news of Christ if we first express it through loving actions that respond to the needs of people, having faith that opportunities to share the motivations for those actions will come.

What Does It Mean for us?

There are many different ways in which we can show our concern for others both as individuals and as congregations. Some practical ideas follow.

Showing Concern as an Individual

As already discussed, choose words which convey empathy more than sympathy. Open yourself up to others sufficiently that you do feel their hurts with them and celebrate their joys with them.

Write short notes or cards to let people know you are thinking about them. Keep a supply of cards or notepaper on hand to make it easier to send notes to neighbors and coworkers who are going through times of sickness, grief, or other difficulties.

Pray for people during a daily devotional time. Share with God your concerns about the needs of those with whom you come in contact. Pray for those persons whom you would especially like to reach with the Christian message or invite to church. Seek God's guidance in recognizing appropriate opportunities to talk about your faith or to invite them to an event in your congregation.

Network on behalf of your friends. When you have friends who are experiencing problems, do what Connie and Bob did for Michael by networking. Get on the phone to people you know who may know someone else who can be of help – no matter what the problem is. Obviously you want to keep your integrity with those with whom you network; don't make promises about the person you seek to help if you aren't sure they are true. But it isn't necessary to know the life story of a new friend in order to make a few contacts on behalf of that person.

Invite people to share a meal with you. One of the most concrete ways of showing that you care is by inviting someone to share a meal with you at a restaurant or in your home. That's what Connie and Bob did for Michael, and it made a positive difference in all of their lives. Don't look too narrowly when deciding what persons to invite into your home or your social life – some of your very best experiences may come with persons who are considerably older or considerably younger than yourself; with persons of different ethnic background; with persons of different educational or economic background; and with persons of different marital status. Single people, including single parents, often feel painfully shut off from the lives of married couples.

Invite a mix of people into your home. At least a couple of times a year, invite a mixture of your friends from church and of the friends you would like involved in your church to your home for a meal or party. Valentine's Day, Groundhog Day, Superbowl Sunday, the Christmas season, or no occasion at all can give you an opportunity to let people interact.

Showing Concern as a Congregation

Have children's classes make "welcoming wreaths." Have the children use raffia ribbon to make the wreaths and encourage them to give their creations to new households in their neighborhood or to elderly persons.

Sponsor a Mother's Day Out. On Saturdays at your church, offer games and child care while mothers have opportunity to shop and run errands. Have literature on your church available which explains why you offer such services.

Take Polaroid pictures in parks. Organize your church to have volunteers take Polaroid photographs of children and families in parks during the summer. Give the photographs to people at no charge. Put a sticker on the back which says something like:

> *This is given to you as a gift*
> *by the members of:*
>
> **First United Community Church**
> **2030 Forest Park Drive**
> **809-555-2344**
>
> *We seek to serve the community*
> *in Christ's name. If we can ever*
> *be of help to you for any reason,*
> *please call us.*

Distribute devotional booklets. Have members of the congregation write short (one page) devotions, modeled after those which appear in *The Upper Room*, for the Easter or Christmas seasons. Distribute these booklets broadly in the community as a service. These could also cause some people to decide they want to visit your congregation!

For other strategies to pursue, you'll find lots of help in *Fifty Ways You Can Share Your Faith* by Tony Campolo and Gordon Aeschliman. The book is a refreshing change of pace from most treatments of evangelism, and the ideas are practical.

 Codependency:

Bookstores and lecture circuits are filled with counsel on the trap of codependency, in which we become a part of unhealthy relationships rather than truly helping others. The term codependency is sometimes overused, causing helpful Christian behavior to be identified as codependent when it is not. On the other hand, some churches have encouraged a style of service which is really glorified codependency.

We do need to avoid caring behaviors which:

- *Attempt to "rescue" others, making ourselves into saviors rather than pointing people to Christ and their own strength.*

- *Keep another person from taking responsibility for his or her own behavior and its consequences.*

- *Help other people with their problems as an escape from facing our own problems.*

Some Things to Try

1. Think about the needs in your own life in relationship to the categories of Maslow and Glasser. In which areas do your own needs seem to be well met? In which areas do you need some work or some help in order to do a better job and to feel better about your own life? Remember that it is difficult for us to be kind to others if we are ourselves extremely dissatisfied.

2. Complete "The Caring Response" exercise at the end of this chapter. In that exercise, some possible first responses are provided to problems or concerns of others. In each instance, decide which response feels most comfortable and natural to you. As you go through the exercise, be alert for instances in which it's possible to express a deeper identification through empathy than sympathy.

Some responses (such as one referring to the loss of your own parents) may not be possible if you have not yet had the described experience. In those instances where a specific action is suggested, think about whether or not that action response would be a comfortable or viable one for you personally to make.

There are no "right" or "wrong" answers to the exercise, but some answers may seem more appropriate than others in terms of sharing genuine concern and leaving the door open for future connecting points or deeper sharing.

The purpose of the exercise is to help us think more carefully about the kind of responses that we make (or fail to make). In each instance, in reality, the reactions of the other person to your words and actions would determine much of your response.

The Caring Response

1. You are visiting with a coworker who shares with you that
   he still feels considerable emptiness and sometimes outright
   pain over the death of his father three months ago. The
   father had lived out of state, and you had not known about
   the death at the time it occurred.

   ___ a. "I'm sorry to learn of his death. I would have shared
   my sympathy for you at the time if I had known
   about it. Had he been ill for a long time?"

   ___ b. "I can identify some with what you're feeling. No
   two situations are the same; but my father died two
   years ago, and I still feel a great deal of emptiness."

   ___ c. "I'm sorry to learn you've had such a significant
   loss. I can't even imagine what it would feel like
   to lose a parent."

   ___ d. "I'm sorry you've experienced such a loss. Is there
   anything I can do here at the office to help take
   pressure off of you during this difficult time?"

   ___ e. "A loss like that is always a great one. If your
   father was a believer, you at least have the assurance
   that he is now in heaven."

   ___ f. Other: _____

2. You learn from a next-door neighbor that a man who lives
   a few doors down the street was taken to the hospital for
   a heart attack. Your next-door neighbor tells you that the
   man's wife is home with the children for a couple of hours.
   While you are not well-acquainted with the family down
   the street, you have been visiting with them some about
   neighborhood matters. You know that they were involved
   in a church in their last community but that they haven't
   become involved since moving. You've invited them to
   your church, but they haven't accepted the invitation yet.

   ___ a. Being respectful of their privacy and the pressure
   she must be under, don't make a call on her right
   now. Write a note to her and send another one
   to him at the hospital, letting them know they are
   in your prayers.

   ___ b. Go to her house and say something like, "I just
   wanted to take a moment to express my concern
   about your husband and to ask if there was anything I could do to be of help."

___ c. Go to her house and say something like, "I just wanted to take a moment to express my concern about your husband. I don't want to impose, but I'd be glad to stay with your children for a few hours tonight or some other time if that would be of help. I'm also sure our pastor would be glad to call on your husband in the hospital."

___ d. Communicate the same message as "b" by phone.

___ e. Communicate the same message as "c" by phone.

___ f. Other: _____

3. You are visiting with a friend (who is not involved in a church) who tells you that she and her husband are talking about the possibility of a divorce.

___ a. "I'm so sorry to hear that. Let's pray about it together."

___ b. "A divorce is an awful thing. I hope you don't have to go through that. Have you been getting any counseling?"

___ c. "Having that kind of strain must be very difficult for you. I can't imagine what it must be like to be living with that tension."

___ d. "I can identify with some of the pain you must be feeling. We've come through some difficult times in our marriage. For me, at least, it became hard to think about anything except the tension in the marriage."

___ e. Other: _____

4. The teenager who mows your lawn and seems to enjoy visiting with you shares that she thinks her mother, with whom she lives during the week (with her father on the weekends), is going to get married again soon. The teenager confides that she doesn't like the person her mother plans to marry but also doesn't want to live with her father all the time because of his sporadic drinking problems.

___ a. "That sounds like a very tough situation for you. Tell me more about what you're feeling."

___ b. "Have you tried talking to your mother about what you're feeling?"

___ c. "I'm sure sorry that you're in such a difficult situation. How do you think life at your mother's home will change?"

___ d. Other: _____

Chapter Seven
In Over Our Heads

Concept: In our efforts to help others, we may encounter situations in which the person will be best served by referral to another individual or organization.

Sharon, a nineteen-year-old woman trying to recover from alcoholism, called me at 10 P.M. Her slurred speech and almost incoherent conversation made it apparent that she was not doing well with her recovery that evening. From past experience, I had learned that visiting with an alcoholic who was already drunk is like closing a barn door after the horse is gone. Yet I didn't feel comfortable ending this particular conversation with her too quickly.

As she talked, I soon learned this was not an ordinary drunk. In a suicide attempt, Sharon had washed down a handful of pills with alcohol. I could not handle the situation on my own – she needed medical help immediately. I learned she was calling from a public telephone in a local fast-food restaurant. I told her that I had something very important to do, got her telephone number, and promised to call her back in a few minutes. As soon as I hung up, I dialed the local ambulance service, explained what she had done, and told them where she was.

I then called Sharon back and visited with her until the EMTs arrived. When she saw them coming, she cursed at me for calling them and violating her confidentiality. I felt guilty but also felt I had done what was necessary to save her life. The next day, when I visited her in the hospital, a repentant Sharon thanked me for the help.

As Christians, we listen carefully to others, express our concern, and respond to their needs when appropriate. In that process, we may discover crucial needs which we can't handle alone. Some situations require experience, professional training, or authority which we do not have.

Accepting Limitations

Mark 9:14-29 describes what happened after Jesus, Peter, James, and John came down from the mountain after the Transfiguration. A frustrated father had approached the other nine disciples with a son who suffered from seizures. Today the son would probably be considered epileptic; but at that time, possession by a spirit was thought to be the cause. At an earlier time, Jesus had instructed the disciples to cast out unclean spirits, and they had experienced some success [Mark 6:7,13]. This time, however, they were totally ineffective.

A crowd had gathered and a group of scribes in the crowd saw this failure of the disciples as an opportunity to criticize Jesus and his followers. The scribes and the disciples were in the middle of an argument when Jesus and the other three disciples arrived. No one deals easily with the verbal attacks of others, and it's easy to become as caught up in arguments as the disciples were. Our natural inclination when criticized is to feel guilty or to become defensive.

While the debate raged between the scribes and the disciples, the frantic father wondered if anyone could help his epileptic son. In the face of a crisis, we can be tempted to debate, argue, discuss, blame, and analyze. At such times, we need to respond to the situation, even if our solution is less than ideal. Any helpful action for the one who suffers is preferable to preoccupation with our own emotions or to debate over what went wrong.

The distressed father explained to Jesus what had taken place. The father then asked Jesus to help, "if you are able." Hearing the word *if* made Jesus realize the man's faith needed to be strengthened. Jesus questioned the father about his faith in the power of God. The father became the first person in the story to admit his own limitations as he proclaimed: "I believe; help my unbelief!" [verse 25].

Jesus called for the unclean spirit to leave the boy. The child shook with convulsions and then went into a coma-like state. Although some in the crowd thought the boy was dead, Jesus calmly took his hand and lifted him up – completely healed.

The final verses of this passage describe a private discussion Jesus had with the disciples about their ineffectiveness in healing the boy. Jesus explained: "This kind can only come out through prayer" [verse 29]. Jesus did not provide a magic formula for future encounters with unclean spirits but pointed to the necessity of communion with and trust in an all-powerful God. There are two reasons why Jesus was effective when the disciples were not:

First, Jesus had authority the disciples did not. They spoke as followers of the hoped-for Messiah, but he spoke with the authority of the Son of God. We need to acknowledge that there are situations in which some people have more implicit authority than others. For example, how can a woman who is five foot two and weighs only 110 pounds stop a bus going forty miles per hour with one hand? The answer is simple: she needs to be wearing a police uniform. That uniform gives her authority that causes the bus driver to stop when she raises her hand.

Second, Jesus had skills that the disciples did not. In attempting to help others, we need to recognize our limitations. With serious physical illness, for example, we reach a point at which we give up on self-medication and call for help. Turning to the right person can also be important. When sick, we call a physician rather than a plumber. When our pipes are broken and the basement is flooded, we call a plumber rather than a physician.

Practicing Humility

With most problems people discuss with us, a willingness to listen and a desire to express our concern as appropriate will be effective responses. Some situations, however, call for skills and expertise we do not have:

1. When there is a medical emergency: This could include a suicide attempt, a sexually transmitted disease, untreated severe illness, or untreated severe physical injuries.

2. When the person is suicidal: If the person expresses strong feelings of hopelessness and talks about giving up, we need to ask directly: "Are you thinking about hurting yourself?" By asking this question, we are not putting ideas in the person's head. If the individual is suicidal, he or she will have thought about it long before the question. If the answer is "yes," immediate referral is indicated unless one has had professional training in handling such situations.

3. When the person is involved in alcohol or drug abuse: Those who fall victim to chemical abuse or dependency are in the clutches of a cunning, baffling, and powerful force. In addition, the person may be in denial about the seriousness of his or her chemical abuse. To break through this, we need to ask very specific questions (without condemnation) about the person's alcohol and/or drug use. If we suspect a problem, we need to refer the person to someone who can correctly assess the situation and provide the appropriate professional help.

4. When the person is suffering from physical or emotional abuse: This could apply to child abuse, spouse abuse, or elderly abuse by caregivers. Weak excuses for bruises can be an indication of physical abuse. A very low self-esteem coupled with a high dependency on or rebellion toward a certain person are indicators of emotional abuse. Protecting the person from further physical or emotional abuse takes precedence over other considerations. Refer this person immediately.

5. When the person has suffered rape or sexual abuse: A person will not share an incident or history of rape or of sexual abuse with us unless we have developed a high degree of trust in the relationship. Rape or sexual abuse results in an enormous amount of emotional damage. Even if the event or events occurred a long time ago, deep emotional scars often remain. Only someone with professional training can help the victim deal with these deep hurts.

6. When the person has legal problems: These could be either criminal or civil difficulties. It's frighteningly easy to give a person bad advice because of how cousin Harold dealt with a similar situation (which may actually be very different). We should resist the temptation to give legal advice unless we have attended law school!

7. When there are complicated family problems: When there are patterns of repeated unhealthy behavior within a family, the underlying dysfunctional dynamics can be extremely complex. Such family situations are sometimes made even worse by factors like alcohol abuse, physical abuse, or chronic low self-esteem for some family members. Experienced marriage and family counselors are generally needed to deal effectively with such situations.

8. When we feel like we are in over our heads: Occasionally the person one seeks to help has not identified any of the preceding problems, but one still feels ineffective in giving support. In these circumstances, one may feel drained or heavily burdened whenever talking with that person. When we repeatedly have such feelings, a referral should be made to someone who can deal with the person more objectively.

Where Do We Refer?

The question then becomes, to where do we refer? If you are a lay person, you may wish to start by consulting with your pastor. Most clergy have an extensive file of good referral resources. If your pastor does not know where to refer, many telephone books have sections listing helping services in the area. Some communities publish human service directories listing referral sources by specific problem areas. There are some common referral resources which most communities have. These include:

• **Medical resources such as doctors, emergency rooms, health departments, and free clinics.** It might be wise to identify which doctor or medical resource would have special skill or resources in dealing with specific problems areas.

• **Self-help and 12-step programs** such as Alcoholics Anonymous, Narcotics Anonymous, Alanon (for family members of chemical abusers), Overeaters Anonymous, and Toughlove. All of these are excellent, and most have printed schedules they are willing to give anyone who is interested.

• **Trained counselors and community mental health centers.** Individual professionals and private or public agencies can offer individual, marriage, family, and group counseling. Again it is good to know specific areas of expertise before making a referral.

• **Specific agencies which deal with abuse or neglect.** County-run departments which deal with the abuse or neglect of a minor may call themselves such things as human services, family services, child protection services, or child welfare. In the case of spouse abuse, many communities have shelter houses or agencies to protect and work with the victim. There are also agencies to help when a caregiver is suspected of abusing an elderly person.

How does one make a good referral? Here are some specific steps to take:

1. You need to reassure the person that you will continue to be there for him or her as a friend. In that context, you need to explain that help is needed beyond what you can provide. Explain what the professional, the agency or organization, or the self-help group may be able to accomplish. Be sure that your friendship and support of the person do not stop with the referral.

2. You should walk the person through the steps of making an appointment or finding out a meeting time. When making a referral, it's best to immediately go to a telephone and help the person make the call. There are many people who promise to "call them later" but never get around to it.

3. You should consider going with the person to the first appointment or self-help meeting. This does not necessarily mean attending the meeting or going in for the actual appointment with the professional. It may mean providing transportation and staying in the waiting room during an appointment.

4. If you do not accompany the person to the initial appointment or meeting, check back later to find out how it went. If the person is happy with the referral, you can provide encouragement. If referral did not work well, you may need to help the person find a more acceptable alternative.

5. There are times the person will refuse the referral no matter how badly it is needed. In some situations, you need to simply let it go and continue to pray for and support the person. Perhaps he or she is not yet ready to deal with these issues. In a small number of cases, to be discussed below, you may not be able to responsibly "let it go" because of the very real danger of the person's immediate situation.

As suggested in the fifth point, there are some cases in which we can't simply drop the matter if the person refuses to accept the referral. We can't walk away if the person is in imminent danger because of suicidal thoughts, physical abuse or neglect, sexual abuse or rape, physical problems arising from alcohol or drug abuse, or sexually transmitted diseases. If the person is in that kind of danger and refuses referral, then we need to firmly share our own anxiety and sense of responsibility over the individual's welfare. We need to explain that we may have to violate the person's confidentiality in order to provide help but that we would prefer not being in that bind. Enlist the person as a partner in the difficult situation that has been created because of the information which has been shared.

Of course the emergency nature of some situations or the physical or emotional state of the person seeking help from us may preclude the kind of reasoned discussion one would like to have. That was the case, for example, in the situation I described at the beginning of this chapter. There may be rare occasions, like that one, when we feel called to violate confidentiality and notify a close family member or the proper authority. When we violate confidentiality in these cases, the person may become very angry with us; but if we save that person's life or prevent serious physical harm, it's an anger worth enduring. The person helped will often feel better about our actions at a future, calmer time.

If a person asks about confidentiality during a discussion, it is important to be honest in the response which is made. You might want to say something like: "As your friend, I will respect your confidentiality completely unless it appears you are in imminent danger from yourself or someone else. In that situation, my preference would be that we agree together on what to do about the seriousness of the problem rather than my being forced to consider violating your confidentiality."

If you are a minister, an educator, a psychologist, a physician, a social worker, or another professional person whose interaction with the person being helped could be construed as a professional interaction, you may be under legal obligation to report certain kinds of situations. A full consideration of the legal issues related to confidentiality goes beyond the scope of this book, which is focused on sharing in the context of friendship, but professional persons want to stay aware of laws which affect their relationships with others.

It's difficult to overemphasize how important confidentiality is when people share feelings, experience, fears, or hopes which are clearly intended only for our ears. We need to be extremely careful that we don't inadvertently violate their trust by sharing something with another friend in the church community, a friend we have in common with the person being helped, or even a member of one's own household. Nothing destroys the trust in a relationship more quickly than the failure to keep a confidence, and the circumstances when we should violate that trust are very few in number.

Some Things To Try

1. At the end of this chapter, you'll find a worksheet titled "Common Places to Make Referrals." Spend some time talking with your pastor or going through the telephone book or an area helping services directory in order to identify available resources. Decide on the ones which would be most useful for the sorts of situations you would feel most likely to encounter as a result of reaching out to others. Call these places and find out: (a) what

services they have available, (b) at what hours, (c) at what fees, and (d) how to make a referral to them. Record the basic information in the space provided on that page, or create your own one-page directory to tape inside your telephone book or address book so that it is readily available.

2. This chapter indicated that there are times we feel "in over our heads" even though the problems a person is experiencing do not fit the criteria suggested for referral. Write down some of the situations which would cause you to feel heavily burdened. Try to identify why you have these feelings. Remember that feelings as such are not *good* or *bad*. We simply need to identify them without any negative judgment on ourselves and endeavor to understand them as best we can.

Common Places to Make Referrals

In each of the following categories, identify referral sources available in your area and find out: (1) what services they have available, (2) at what hours, (3) at what fees, and (4) how to make referrals to them.

Medical Resources:

Self-help Groups:

Trained Counselors and Mental Health Centers:

Agencies Dealing with Abuse and Neglect Issues (of minors, spouses, and elderly):

Chapter Eight
Putting It Into Words

Concept: We need to learn how to share
our faith using everyday language rather
than religious jargon or a canned formula.

I first encountered a variation of the story which follows in
the newsletter of a Lutheran congregation in Colorado. I do not
know the original source, but I share my own version here as an
illustration of the problems inherent in communication:

> *Shortly after a woman moved into a new neighborhood,
> she met one of the older residents on the street. "Neighbor,"
> the older resident asked, "do you have salvation?"*
>
> *"Why no," the woman said, "but I'm sometimes bothered
> by arthritis."*
>
> *"You mean you're lost?" the older resident asked.*
>
> *"No, I'm not lost. I live right up the street."*
>
> *"Well, tell me," said the older resident, "are you ready for
> Judgment Day? It's coming real soon now. It may be
> tomorrow or the next day!"*
>
> *"No, I'm not," replied the woman. "And for goodness sake,
> don't tell my husband about it; or he'll want to go both days."*

As Christians, we have access to the most important news in
the world. When we talk about it, however, we often use words
and phrases which are alien to those who need to hear it most.

Salvation, lost, and *Judgment Day* have clear meaning to many of us in the church, but the words are often not clear to persons outside the Christian community.

Some friends have never been to Sunday School or church. Some neighbors have never read the Bible. Some relatives have never discussed religious issues with anyone. Yet we assume those we talk with about our faith are familiar with these topics and fluent in biblical terminology. When we make such assumptions, we create a barrier between ourselves and those we want to reach.

If we are going to be successful at putting our faith into words, **we need to use our own words** – not the words of the Apostle Paul or a popular theologian. We need to use the same words we would in a normal conversation on another topic. When we use words that are not natural to us, our conversation becomes stilted and our relationships artificial.

The Light of the World

In **Matthew 5:14-16**, near the beginning of the Sermon on the Mount, Jesus affirms his followers by calling them "the light of the world." He then talks about sharing the light with everyone in the house by putting it on a lampstand and not under a bushel basket.

Many families in Palestine in the time of Jesus lived in one-room homes which had only one eighteen-inch round window. Consequently, it was dark even in the daytime; and families often kept a lamp burning twenty-four hours a day. The lamp consisted of a bowl of oil with a wick floating in it, and the bowl was placed on a lampstand. During the day, when the family was gone, a clay bushel-basket was commonly put over the lamp to keep it from causing a fire. When family members returned, the basket was removed, and the lamp became the principle source of light in the home.

Virtually all of us have walked into a dark house when the electricity was out. We grope around with our hands and move very slowly and carefully. Almost without fail, we find something to run into or, even worse, trip over. The return of electric power brings a pleasant sense of relief.

Can you imagine intentionally walking around a dark house without turning on the lights? You wouldn't unless you were concerned about waking someone. Can you imagine entertaining guests and refusing to turn on the lights? You wouldn't unless it was a surprise party, and you were waiting on the guest of honor. Some of us, however, entertain close friends without turning on the light of Jesus Christ. That light helps people see themselves, others, and their surroundings with far greater clarity. Do we want to have friendships which are so superficial that we never share what Christ and the church mean in our lives?

Perhaps we are hesitant to turn on "spiritual lights" because we are afraid that our own light is too dim to be of help. We need to remember that we are sharing not our own light but the light of Jesus Christ. Paul writes to the church at Corinth:

> *For it is the God who said, "Let light shine out of darkness," who has shone in our hearts to give the light of the knowledge of the glory of God in the face of Jesus Christ.*
> **2 Corinthians 4:6**

In **Matthew 7:15-29**, the conclusion of the Sermon on the Mount, Jesus reminds us of our need to witness with good works, which are referred to in the New Revised Standard translation as *good fruit.* The Greek word for "good" in this passage doesn't describe a hard, cold, severe goodness, but a warm, attractive, lovely goodness. To have integrity, our witness to the gospel needs to be supported by our works. Francis of Assisi urged us to: "Preach the gospel at all times. If necessary, use words."

Does Jesus Give Us the Words to Speak?

In **Matthew 10:16-23**, Jesus warned the disciples about inevitable persecution once they began sharing the good news of the kingdom. They would be brought before councils, governors, and kings. To prepare the disciples for these difficult situations, Jesus reassured them: "When they hand you over, do not worry about how you are to speak or what you are to say; for what you are to say will be given to you at the time; for it is not you who speak, but the Spirit of your Father speaking through you" [verses 19-20].

Most of us have not been brought before councils, governors, and kings because of our religious faith. Nothing suggested in this book is likely to cause that to happen! If one follows the suggested stages of this book, then the faith-sharing which one does will be with a person who is ready to listen, prone to be receptive to the message we want to share.

There is always the possibility, of course, of misreading the readiness of another person to hear about our faith or our church. In addition, the process of faith–sharing may raise painful memories for the individual we are seeking to reach. We need to remember that most negative reactions to religious discussions come out of an unpleasant or traumatic experience in the person's past. Many hurtful words and actions have come in the name of Christ. People may have gone through unpleasant experiences in the church, may have been the objects of religious manipulation by a friend or family member, or may have been put down for holding beliefs or opinions which were unorthodox from the perspective of others.

If someone responds to us in an argumentative or resentful way, the natural tendency is to become argumentative or defensive ourselves. That can escalate the conflict and damage the relationship. A healthier response is to:

---

1. Apologize to the person for how he or she has been mentally, emotionally, or spiritually abused by religious people and institutions in the past.

2. Calmly respond to the person's questions, concerns, and opinions.

3. Gently clarify and correct any misconceptions the person may have about the Christian faith.

God will help us respond to the other person. This does not mean we should expect God to intervene with the precise words each time we talk with someone about our faith and the church. The circumstances shared in the tenth chapter of Matthew are the uncommon situations, when we are under stress and have no past experience to adequately prepare us for the present. The passage does not excuse us from building our own faith through prayer and Bible study or from learning how to better express our faith. What this passage does point toward is the reality of God's presence through the Holy Spirit in the midst of our lives and in all the situations we encounter. God is always present when we are engaged in conversation with another person.

Whenever we are talking about our faith, we should offer at least a quick, silent prayer before and even during the conversation. After the discussion, we should offer a prayer of thanksgiving for God's presence and help. We should be especially thankful if the dialogue with the other person included questions for which we could not identify an adequate response, yet we still ended up saying what was needed to open up doors or turn things around. In such circumstances, God has given us the right words.

Putting Faith into Words

Putting our faith into words depends on three factors:

1. Our relationship with the person.
2. Timing.
3. Using words that can be understood.

Some of us find it difficult to converse with a stranger even about relatively superficial things. It's not surprising that talking about our faith is neither natural nor comfortable with an unfamiliar person. In New Testament times, most faith–sharing happened from friend to friend, neighbor to neighbor, and relative to relative.

There are, of course, occasional circumstances when we encounter a stranger who does want to discuss personal problems or religious issues precisely because of the absence of past history between us and, when aboard an airplane for example, the low probability of future association. These situations nevertheless remain the exception. Unless we feel a strong and specific leading of the Holy Spirit, it is ill-advised to talk about faith with strangers. In the absence of an established relationship, we may do more harm than good.

1. Most faith–sharing needs to take place in relationships we have nurtured. We need to have been good listeners, we need to have taken our relationship to deeper levels of communication, and we need to have demonstrated clearly that we care for the other person. In this context, faith–sharing becomes a natural part of conversation. As a result, the discussion avoids feeling forced, awkward, or unnatural.

2. We need to choose a comfortable time and setting to share our faith. Sharing our faith in group settings usually results in intellectual discussions and debates, but real faith affects us at far more than the intellectual level. Unless the group has a high level of openness and past experience in sharing matters of the heart, faith–sharing is best done in one-to-one conversations. It is also better if not done on the run or in the course of a too casual conversation. Faith–sharing is most natural and helpful when the person is already talking about a major life issue.

[Sharing our faith with others in Sunday school or other church groups, of course, is both appropriate and helpful. The above caution about group settings refers to conversations with unchurched people.]

Church growth studies confirm that people are most receptive to invitations to attend church and to discussion of spiritual issues at major junctures or transitions in their lives. Such junctures include:

- Marriage
- Moving
- Changing jobs
- The death of a loved one
- Divorce
- The birth of a child
- Problems with a child
- Major illness or hospitalization

- Changes in the family structure, such as a child going to school for the first time or a teenager going to college

In the midst of such transitions, people are often striving to better understand their lives and are open to new perspectives. People who normally think very little about the meaning of life or their relationships with God may find their minds pulled in those directions by the transitional event. This can make them far more open than usual to faith–sharing and to invitations to attend church.

Faith–sharing with a person is not a one-time experience. Initial conversations may be short and exploratory. Deepening the level of sharing can require more time and trust. A significant life-changing faith conversation may happen only after several prior discussions about faith or the church.

3. We need to share our faith in language unchurched persons can readily understand. Even in religious circles, we are often guilty of throwing around biblical and theological terms which few people fully comprehend. Using those same words with unchurched persons will make it difficult for them to receive our message. Better understanding some biblical terms can help us select words of our own:

- The biblical word for "saved" literally means healed or made whole. People may not understand the word salvation, but they know about **brokenness** and **wholeness**.

- The biblical word for "sin" literally means missing the mark. People may get upset and defensive when we use the word sin, but they understand concepts like **failures** and **shortcomings**.

- The biblical word for "gospel" literally mean good news. The word gospel sounds alien to most secular minds, but everyone is ready to hear **good news**.

- The biblical word for "holy" literally means to be set apart. People may feel perplexed or put off by words like holiness and righteousness, but we all want to be **special** and **set apart in someone's eyes**, especially if that someone is God.

- The biblical word for "evangelism" literally means sharing good news. Many people cringe when they hear the word evangelism because of the mental images or memories brought to mind, but they are happy to **share good news**.

Some words gain force in specific circumstances. The word **lost** can be powerful with people who feel messed up, confused, or overwhelmed. Twelve-step programs teach us some wonderful words to understand our spiritual condition by:

- Calling "grace" a **gift**
- Identifying our "sinful nature" as **defects of character**
- Referring to the "born again" experience as a **spiritual awakening**

For people familiar with popular psychology, words like stress, dysfunctional, self-worth, and self-actualization may be helpful in talking about the human condition. The appropriateness of those and of many other words depends on whether or not they are natural to both persons sharing in conversation.

The Apostle Paul did not hesitate to change words to improve understanding. With one group he emphasized the word *salvation*, with another group the word *redemption*, and with yet another group the word *reconciliation*. He justified this by saying: "I have become all things to all people, that I might by all means save some" [1 Corinthians 9:22].

Some Things To Try

1. At the end of this chapter is an exercise on "Talking about Your Faith." For each area of faith listed, write what that concept means to you – using your own words, not religious jargon.

2. On a piece of paper, identify two or three biblical passages which have been significant in your faith journey. Write your understanding of these Scriptures in your own words, including why each passage has been helpful to you.

3. Prayerfully identify three to five people with whom you might feel reasonably comfortable talking about faith issues. Identify the qualities of your relationship with each person which would help make a faith conversation natural and comfortable. Pray for an opportunity to engage one or two of these people in faith–sharing conversations.

Talking about Your Faith

*Write your beliefs about the following faith concepts using words
understandable to one who has never attended church.*

God is:

Jesus is:

The Holy Spirit is:

Salvation is:

Heaven is:

Hell is:

Praying is:

Real love is:

The church is:

God is present in my life when:

Chapter Nine
When Weakness
Becomes Strength

Concept: Our strongest witness often comes
out of weakness, not strength. People outside
the church are impacted more by a testimony
growing out of difficulty than accomplishment.

At almost any given moment in any given day, somewhere in
North America, a person struggling to recover from alcoholism is
listening to these words of hope:

> *Alcoholics Anonymous is a fellowship of men*
> *and women who share their experience, strength,*
> *and hope with each other so that they may solve*
> *their common problem and help others to recover*
> *from alcoholism.*

A person new to recovery can hear those words of encouragement at his or her first AA meeting, whether in Indiana, West
Virginia, Colorado, British Columbia, or Ontario. These are
powerful words of healing.

The words are powerful because they reassure the recovering
person that he or she is not going to hear a sermon, a lecture, or
a condemnation by someone who assumes a position of moral
superiority. Recovery has little to do with moral superiority. It
has more to do with one recovering person sharing with another
recovering person what has been helpful or effective.

As a result, Alcoholics Anonymous has proven more effective in aiding recovery from alcoholism than psychotherapy, any medical treatment, or religious programs. While professionals certainly have made valuable contributions to people recovering from alcoholism, more lives have been transformed by the mutual sharing of "experience, strength, and hope" through AA. The same words provide power for faith–sharing:

- **Experience** has to do with the past: People share how God has helped them through past difficulties.

- **Strength** has to do with the present: People share how God guides and sustains them through present struggles.

- **Hope** has to do with the future: People share how they trust God and his promises to deal with their anxieties and fears about future unknowns.

D.T. Niles said: "Evangelism is one beggar telling another beggar where to find bread." We are all sinners and fall short of the glory of God. Some of us have been fortunate enough to have our lives transformed by forgiveness, grace, and love. We need to share the wonder of that discovery with others.

Paul and Weakness

The Apostle Paul stands as one of the greatest figures in early church history:

- He brought the gospel to much of the Gentile world.

- He articulated a revolutionary theology of grace.

- He oversaw and helped many churches in their early struggles.

Yet as much as he had accomplished, Paul continued to be aware of his past sin, his present weakness, and his total dependence on the hope of the gospel.

In **1 Corinthians 15:8-9**, Paul describes himself as "un-timely born" or "abnormally born." The Greek for this self-description also means miscarried or premature. We can identify at least two reasons for such a negative self-assessment:

> First, Christ had not called him during his Galilean ministry like the other disciples. Paul was called to be an apostle after Pentecost, by a vision of the risen Christ on the road to Damascus.
>
> Second, Paul had persecuted the church. He had held the cloaks for the witnesses when Stephen had been stoned [Acts 7:54-8:1]. Before his conversion, he had been "breathing threats and murder against the disciples of the Lord" [Acts 9:1]. At the time of his conversion, he had been carrying letters from the high priest so that he might arrest Christians and bring them to Jerusalem for trial.

Many of us feel inadequate talking about our faith or inviting others to church because of our feelings of inferiority or the memory of past mistakes. We hesitate in telling others our experience, strength, and hope because we feel that the weak state of our faith disqualifies us from being Christian witnesses. Yet Paul was not consumed by his feelings of inferiority or his past mistakes. Instead of dwelling on his weakness, Paul focused on God's grace in the call to share the gospel. To the church at Ephesus he wrote:

> *Although I am the very least of all the saints, this grace was given to me to bring to the Gentiles the news of the boundless riches of Christ.*　　　**Ephesians 3:8**

As Christians, we are not only saved by grace, but we are also empowered to share our faith with others through that same grace. God never calls us to any task which he does not equip us to do. That is why Paul assured the church at Corinth with these words:

> *And God is able to provide you with every blessing in abundance, so that by always having enough of everything, you may share abundantly in every good work.*
> **2 Corinthians 9:8**

In **2 Corinthians 12:7-10**, Paul lifts up God's grace rather than his own strength or accomplishments. He shares how God's grace has helped him deal with his "thorn in the flesh." We do not know the specific nature of Paul's thorn. Biblical scholars have speculated that it might have been a physical thorn like an eye ailment, malarial fever, or epilepsy, or a spiritual thorn such as doubt or lust. We do, however, know three things about his thorn:

1. It was persistent in tormenting him.

2. He wanted it removed.

3. It gave him an opportunity to discover Christ's power in a new way.

While Paul came to accept the thorn and to rejoice over the power of Christ experienced because of it, the process was not quick or easy. Paul asked three times to be relieved of the thorn, but the Lord's response was:

> *My grace is sufficient for you, for my power is made perfect in weakness.*
> **2 Corinthians 12:8b**

Sometimes as Christians, we may feel that we are called to be "plaster saints" in times of suffering, not displaying the great pain and distress which we feel. Paul had no hesitation in crying out to God and asking for relief. We need to allow ourselves and others to be human in the struggle to reckon with chronic sickness and other problems. While we may not reach the level of acceptance or rejoicing which Paul experienced, we do experience Christ's power during difficult times.

Through his own weakness, Paul came to experience Christ's power; and that became part of the fundamental message which Paul shared with others: "I am content with weaknesses, insults, hardships, persecutions, and calamities for the sake of Christ; for whenever I am weak, then I am strong" [2 Corinthians 12:10]. Paul discovered, as we can in our own lives, that other people are more likely to identify with our weaknesses and struggles than with our strengths and achievements. When we tell how Christ has nurtured and sustained us through such difficult times, we extend hope to others.

While talking openly about our weakness gives strength to our faith–sharing, we do not want the emphasis to be on ourselves, either in terms of weakness or strength. The emphasis needs to be on the power and grace of Christ within us.

The Willingness to Be Vulnerable

When we come to church, we feel expected to put on our "Sunday best," referring to both clothes and temperament. A family can be in a heated argument, displaying scowling faces and spewing nasty words, and then suddenly, by walking through the doors of the church, be transformed into broad smiles and pleasant greetings. This kind of behavior is no doubt part of the hypocrisy about which people outside the church often complain.

Such expectations and habits make it difficult to show vulnerability in a church setting. During joys and concerns at worship, we are more likely to hear about Aunt Martha's upcoming gall bladder surgery than Uncle John's struggle with lust! We are more likely to hear about a brave person fighting with cancer than about brave parents battling their child's drug addiction. This observation in no way diminishes the impor-tance of community prayer and support for the physical concerns of the congregation, but we also need to remember the importance of support and help in the midst of other struggles.

We are not naively advocating that we begin to share our personal struggles with sin during joys and concerns in worship!

While the church at its best should support that kind of sharing, it is usually neither safe nor wise to share some kinds of personal problems in settings other than small support groups. The desire of people for greater openness and support has much to do with the increasing number of churches which are establishing small groups in which openness, accountability, and confidentiality give people a safe place to share their struggles and to risk being vulnerable.

Outside of that kind of small group setting, our congregations really do not encourage vulnerability. Paul's frankness would be downright embarrassing if he started speaking during the joys and concerns time in most contemporary churches! Yet a willingness to be vulnerable is an integral part of faith–sharing. We can witness to our faith more effectively as we:

1. Are aware of our struggles, needs, shortcomings and sins.
2. Experience self-acceptance through God's grace, (Imitate Paul's attitude of "by the grace of God, I am what I am" in 1 Corinthians 15:10).
3. Have a support group or a prayer partner to help us deal with that weakness and be accountable about our struggles.

Acceptance of our weaknesses does not mean resignation to sin or shaming ourselves for our inadequacies. Rather, it means celebrating who we are as children of God – in process. It means a deep, personal acknowledgment that God loves us "warts and all."

Kingdom values are often upside-down. In Christ's kingdom, radical things happen, like the meek inheriting the earth, the last being the first, and servants being greater than those they serve. Therefore, when looking at our vulnerability from a kingdom perspective, often our greatest weakness is our greatest strength. Our greatest weakness may also give us the greatest opportunity for Christ's power to rest in us and work through us.

To translate our vulnerability into a faith–sharing message, we need to take three steps:

1. We need to identify the weaknesses or the difficult times we have experienced which are most likely to be ones with which other persons can identify.

2. We need to recognize the ways in which Christ has strengthened, loved, and guided us as we have dealt with weaknesses or gone through difficult times.

3. We need to choose the words which will best enable us to share both the weaknesses or difficult times and how Christ's power works in our lives.

Those steps will bring us to a strong testimony from God which can be shared with others.

Perhaps you have been through a marriage which failed in spite of your best efforts to save it. You understand the grieving process and all of the emotions that go with divorce. You understand the hurt, loneliness, anger, guilt, shame, and sense of betrayal which are often part of the process. In relating to a nonbelieving neighbor who is going through an experience which produces similar emotions, you can do more than empathize with that person in his or her pain. You can tell your neighbor about Christ's presence, forgiveness, and healing power through the painful process of your divorce.

Divorce, of course, is only one example of the kind of personal experience which can form a basis for sharing how Christ and the church have helped us. The experiences which we share don't have to be spectacular or tragic to be effective. Other possibilities of situations with which our faith or the church may have made a great difference in our lives include:

- Feeling taken for granted by one's parents, spouse, or children.

- Attempting to handle a problem which other people literally cannot understand.

- Going through serious physical illness or recovery from an accident.

- Dealing with the serious illness of a loved one.

- Having a permanent physical disability.

- Living with a person who has a permanent physical disability.

- Handling a painful experience which happened in the church.

- Feeling profoundly unappreciated for the amount one has done for an organization like the church.

- Handling the death of a loved one.

- Struggling with addiction to alcohol or other drugs.

- Living with a loved one who has an addiction to alcohol or other drugs.

- Finding the strength to stop smoking.

- Going through a difficult time with a child.

- Helping an elderly parent.

- Overcoming addiction to work or the pursuit of profit at any cost.

- Going through the loss of a pet to which one had been deeply attached for years.

- Dealing with chronic depression or suicidal thoughts.

- Living with the chronic depression or suicidal thoughts of a loved one.

- Working through an extramarital relationship.

- Having a spouse involved in an extramarital relationship.

- Handling a financial crisis.

- Working on a daily basis in an employment setting filled with tension.

- Going through a period of unemployment.

- Working through the complex emotions following a rape or sexual abuse.

- Being charged with a crime.

- Being a victim of crime.

- Dealing with other serious legal problems.

- Going through a time when God seemed absent from life.

- Living with not being as financially successful as others in one's family or circle of friends.

- Experiencing guilt and anxiety over achieving a spectacular degree of success in a particular area of life.

- Experiencing guilt over having had a life which feels much better than many other people seem to have.

- Handling anger over a life which seems filled with far more tragedy and struggle than others seem to experience.

While we may occasionally share our faith story or a testimony with a congregation or another large group, most of our faith–sharing will be done with only one other person or occasionally with a small group. In some respects, we should think of faith–sharing as scattering seeds. Most people come to Christ only after many seeds have been planted by many individuals on many occasions.

Sharing strategies such as those built on Campus Crusade for Christ's Four Spiritual Laws communicate strong intellectual and spiritual conviction, and we are not arguing against using such strategies. The kind of faith–sharing we have been discussing does have particular power in three ways. First, rather than just dealing with people at the level of opinions, this approach reaches to the level of feelings and deals with people at their points of greatest need. Second, in this kind of vulnerable faith–sharing, we are allowing God to transform our greatest weakness, by grace, into a force for great good. We are living the gospel message in the vulnerable way we share it with others. Third, the words that we use and the examples that we share grow out of our own experience and our own relationships with Christ.

The world in which we live desperately needs the Christian faith and the community of the body of Christ. The Christian faith and community provide greatly needed values in a world which seems to have lost any moral compass. The Christian faith and community provide nurture for diverse people who are seeking to grow in their faith and love for one another. The Christian faith and community can be a vehicle for social and political change in a world hungry for reform. But to another human being who is struggling with his or her own problems and needs, the greatest gift we can provide is the experience, strength, and hope we have found in Jesus Christ.

Some Things To Try

1. At the end of this chapter is an exercise called "Sharing the Real You – Loved By God." It asks you to identify your three greatest strengths, your three greatest weaknesses or short-comings, your three greatest fears, and your three greatest hopes or dreams. After identifying those, prayerfully consider what message you have to give in faith–sharing. Try putting that message into words.

Share this process and your subsequent faith story or testimony with another person in your church, in your family, or in your circle of friends. Invite that person to share in a similar way with you, if he or she is comfortable doing so. Seek feedback on how you came across in the faith–sharing process, and pray for continuing guidance.

2. Prayerfully identify unchurched friends who are going through struggles and dealing with weaknesses similar to those you have experienced. Pray for and be open to an opportunity to

share in a faith discussion with one or more of those friends.

3. In **1 Timothy 1:15-16**, Paul calls himself the worst of sinners! Many of us are reluctant to share our struggles and shortcomings with persons who respect us or whose respect we would like to cultivate. Timothy was Paul's protegee, and yet Paul humbly and openly pointed out his own weaknesses in instructions shared with Timothy. During the coming week, observe the people around you and think about your inter-actions with them. How often does the desire to appear in control or to be respected get in the way of honest communi-cation? How do you feel when someone you respect shows a willingness to be vulnerable? What opportunities for faith–sharing may be present in such situations?

☞ *Look again* at an overview of the faith–sharing process suggested in this book.

We can comfortably relate our faith in Christ to others and invite others into the life of the church through a process of:
- Forming genuine friendships.
- Listening to the needs of our friends and learning to ask deeper questions.
- Caring for our friends and showing that care in words and actions.
- Telling in our own words how Christ and the church have made a difference in our lives, building not so much on our strength or wisdom as on our weakness.
- Inviting others into the life of the congregation.
- Helping those who join the church become fully incorporated into the body of Christ.
- Recognizing that it is Christ who saves and that we must respect where others are in openness to Christ and the church.

The next two chapters talk about strategies to help new people become fully involved in the church, the body of Christ.

☞ ***But*** *what if . . .*

- *You do not feel comfortable with the kind of faith–sharing described in this chapter?*
- *Or you're not sure you feel comfortable with any kind of faith–sharing?*

Then . . .

- *Be patient with yourself. You may grow in comfort with the passage of time.*
- *Remember that you don't necessarily have to share your faith story or testimony on just one dramatic occasion. If you follow the earlier guidelines in this book of listening to others, asking questions, and showing concern, there will be many different opportunities to discuss religious concerns.*
- *Have confidence that the quality of your relationships with others who know that your faith and the church are important to you will be a part of the seeds sown by many, even if you do not come to a point at which you share your faith story.*

And what if . . .

- *You find that most of the unchurched people you know feel that they already are Christians?*

Then . . .

- *Use your opportunities to visit with these persons to show how the Christian faith comes alive for you in the Christian community.*
- *And invite these persons to come to church with you to see for themselves what the Christian community to which you belong is like.*
- *Remember if your invitations are rejected that this does not mean you have failed – only that the other person is not yet ready.*

Sharing the Real You – Loved by God

D.T. Niles has said: "Evangelism is one beggar telling another beggar where to find bread." Talking down to people or preaching at them doesn't usually help. When we share our faith, the emphasis needs to be on God's strength, not our own. Complete the following items to get in better touch with your own strengths, weaknesses, and opportunities for faith-sharing.

My three greatest strengths are:

1.

2.

3.

My three greatest weaknesses or shortcomings are:

1.

2.

3.

My three greatest fears are:

1.

2.

3.

My three greatest hopes and dreams are:

1.

2.

3.

> **The faith story which grows out of my life and feels most comfortable to share with others:**

Chapter Ten
Helping New Friends
Feel Welcome

Concept: If those we bring into the Christian community are truly friends, we will not abandon them at the point of membership, but encourage them to build relationships with others in Christ's body, the church. Congregations need systematic ways of ensuring that all people feel welcome.

Inviting someone to your church may get that person to the doorway, but whether or not that individual comes again depends heavily on what happens after crossing the threshold. The following comments are from persons whose congregational visits were less than ideal experiences:

- "I couldn't believe it. We visited the church three weeks in a row and not a single person gave us more than a hello. It was like we were invisible. During the coffee time that they encouraged visitors to attend, people who already belonged were all in their own little circles talking with each other, and we pretty much just stood by ourselves."

- "Initially I felt warmly received by the people at St. Paul's. We were welcomed every week at worship, and the people in the Sunday school class seemed obviously glad to have us. The pastor called on us right away, and a lay person came to answer questions. But now we've been members for six months, and it's almost like we don't matter anymore. The people there seem to take us for granted now. I know there are people in the class who get together socially, but we're not part of that. People still give us superficial greetings, but there's no depth."

- "We started going to First Church because our good friends Beth and Andrew told us how great the congregation was. We went with them the first time, and it seemed like everything they said was true. Now that we've been there awhile though, some of that initial welcome seems phony. It's almost like a 'come on' to get you in the door, onto the books, and into the pledging system . . . . I don't mean that anyone intentionally did that. Beth and Andrew are sincere, and the other people probably are too, but they're already so involved in the life of the church that it's hard for them to fit new people into the system."

- "We stopped going to Anderson Creek Church. We are probably still on the books as members, but we haven't attended for almost a year. The church is made up primarily of people who've been in that denomination all of their lives, and it feels like half the members belong to about four big families with grandparents, parents, children, grandchildren all part of the congregation. I think the congregation didn't worry about reaching out to anyone until a few years ago, when their membership was declining so much that they could hardly afford a full-time pastor. Their people got all fired up to reach out, and our neighbors who had belonged to the church forever suddenly started inviting us to attend. They talked about how important their faith was to them, and that's really when I accepted Christ in my own life. It was a spiritual high, and I'll always be thankful for the experience . . . .

"But then when we started trying to get truly involved in the church, it became real clear that we were second class citizens. We were good enough to teach a Sunday school class but not to be on the board or the property committee. We'd share opinions on ways it seemed the church could improve how it handled things, and it was made abundantly clear that we hadn't been in the church long enough to understand how things were really done. We finally stopped coming, and no one ever bothered to find out why. Our neighbors still wave to us, but we haven't talked with them about church since they left off the pledge cards last fall."

Sharing the faith with people, inviting them to church, and even getting them to become members of the church are only part of the process in helping them grow in Christ's love. As the preceding examples show, people can feel shut out at many points in their relationship with a congregation. If we care about others, then we want to create an atmosphere in which they will truly feel welcome and will become part of the process of welcoming others.

Stages in Ignoring

There are several stages or points of contact at which new people can feel ignored, overlooked, or even put-down by a congregation:

1. From the start. Although repeated studies show that people in most congregations feel they warmly welcome visitors, the perception of visitors is not always the same. A major national study, which was reported in *Overcoming Barriers to Church Growth* and in *Creating Quality in Ministry*, shared the results of asking both congregational members and visitors to "grade" the church from A (excellent) to F (failing) in terms of its warmth. In almost every church participating in that study, active church members gave the church a full letter grade higher than visitors.

Some visitors have the experience of literally no one speaking to them. That experience seems to happen most frequently either in relatively small congregations in which people are not accustomed to visitors and may even be suspicious of them and in very large congregations in which people almost literally are lost. Visitors need to be greeted by persons in addition to designated greeters and ushers.

An introduction and a warm handshake represent a minimal level of hospitality, but they are not necessarily sufficient. While that may be all for which there's time in the sanctuary before the worship service and as much as some first time visitors want, many visitors will have different expectations. Those expectations are often communicated by visitors going to the fellowship time, lingering in the sanctuary after the service has ended, or waiting until near the last to leave a Sunday school class.

Fellowship times can be the most frustrating for visitors, because so many congregations promote those as an opportunity for visitors to meet members of the church. It's very common during fellowship times for church members to be talking in such tightly knit clusters that visitors are literally shut out and left to stand by themselves. Visitors can legitimately conclude in such a congregation that they are not especially welcome and that church members already have friendship bonds which are too strong for outsiders to penetrate. This situation is a sufficiently serious problem that several churches have initiated programs of "silent greeters," who are persons without any official visitor badge or designation who make it their task to see that people mix during the fellowship time and that visitors do get introduced to church members on a one-to-one or family-to-family basis.

2. Third, fourth, fifth, or sixth visit. The initial warmth of the congregation may seem quite genuine and welcoming to visitors, but sometimes that impression fades over the next few visits. Most visitors do not, for example, expect that their names will be remembered by everyone in the church after only one visit. On the other hand, if they have had two or three conversations with class members or with people during a fellowship time and still find that those persons do not know their names, they have understandable reason to wonder how much difference their presence makes.

Those who start to attend a Sunday school class or a small group may become aware that several others in the class or group are accustomed to meeting socially outside of the regular meeting time. One of the major motivations for attending church is a desire to share in community with other Christians, to have a sense of actively participating in the body of Christ. While some people who visit already have strong networks of friends, many do not. Even those who do have established friendship networks generally want to form new friendships within the Christian community. When you have the sense that others are participating in social events from which you are excluded, your sense of welcome inevitably declines.

Some churches have a systematic program which works well to respond to the initial visit by new people, but those congregations aren't necessarily sure what to do when a person keeps coming. As people continue to attend, they often have more questions about Sunday school classes, choirs, small group opportunities, and other aspects of the life of the church. When no one is staying in regular contact, they may not be certain how to get the information. Visitors who are extroverted will obviously start asking questions of anyone who is available or take the initiative to call the persons who first invited them, but not all persons are comfortable being that socially assertive.

3. After joining. In most congregations, people do not become thoroughly assimilated or incorporated into the body of Christ until well after they've formally become members. They still have the need to develop deeper relationships within the congregation, the need to find meaningful places to serve in the life of the church, and the need to feel that their presence is making a difference. Substantial numbers of people join churches each year only to become inactive before another year has passed.

What's It Like to Visit?

Try a mental exercise to better understand how visitors, especially those with no past connection to a local church, feel when they attend for the first time. Suppose that good Jewish friends of yours have been encouraging you to attend a service at the synagogue where they worship. Think about the kinds of questions you're likely to experience in the process of making that visit:

- Where do you park? Are some of the places reserved?

- Where do you enter the building? You may see
  people going in at three or four different entrances.

- As you encounter people, should you be taking the initiative at introducing yourself? Should you leave that to the people you encounter? Will you be thought cold if you don't introduce yourself? Will you be thought too forward if you do?

- Where are the restrooms? How comfortable do you feel asking someone for directions?

- If you have a young child, what's the condition of the nursery? Do you feel comfortable leaving your child there? What kind of reassurance would make you feel all right about that?

- Do you want to sign the registration book? What will happen if you sign it and give your address? Will the rabbi be at your front door in twelve hours?

- How on earth can you follow the service of worship? Why are some people wearing head coverings but others are not doing so?

- Is an offering going to be taken? If one is, what amount is appropriate for a visitor to donate?

- Is it all right to whisper to someone else (like your spouse who is drifting into sleep or your child who is contemplating throwing the paper airplane which has just been created from the synagogue's program)?

- What do you do when it becomes apparent that some people are introducing themselves to the whole congregation? Do you want to stand up and introduce yourself?

- Do you want to wear a name tag? Does that make it more likely that people will greet you? If it does make it more likely, does that feel positive or negative to you?

- How familiar are the biblical passages to which the rabbi refers in the message? Does lack of familiarity with Old Testament passages and with the Jewish culture make it difficult for you to follow all of the message?

* Do you want a visit within a couple of days from the rabbi or from another person in the synagogue?

* What anxieties are produced from simply contemplating the experience? Are you a person made more curious by lack of knowledge, or are you more likely to avoid situations which you've not experienced before?

If you've had several occasions to visit synagogues and already feel comfortable doing so, then think about another congregation which is rather different than your own. That could be a Roman Catholic congregation, a more fundamentalist congregation than the one you attend, a congregation of your own denomination located in an inner city neighborhood or by a college campus, a more liberal or mainline congregation than the one you attend, or even a "new age" congregation. Think through the issues involved and consider the possibility of actually attending such a congregation for the value of what you would learn out of the experience.

Did Ananias Want to Welcome Paul?

The ninth chapter of Acts tells the story of Paul's encounter with Christ on the Damascus Road. As a consequence of that experience, Paul was unable to see. The Lord came to Ananias in a vision, urging him to go to Paul (still referred to as Saul in the biblical text) and lay hands on him. [You may wish to read **Acts 9:1-22**.]

Ananias obviously wasn't pleased by the vision and reminded God of Paul's reputation (as though God needs reminding!): "Lord, I have heard from many about this man, how much evil he has done to your saints in Jerusalem; and here he has authority to bind all who invoke his name." Ananias didn't feel it was safe to approach Paul, but there's a limit on how much anyone wants to argue with God!

Ananias did in fact go to Paul and served as Christ's messenger both in healing Paul and in helping him become filled with the Holy Spirit and join the Christian community. The fact that Ananias did not initially want to approach or welcome Paul did not remain a barrier to Paul's assimilation into the body of Christ.

Scripture, in fact, places the burden on the believer in terms of how he or she relates to the stranger. Our Lord expected Ananias to reach out to the stranger whose reputation made him seem frightening. The Good Samaritan modeled right conduct and a right relationship with God by caring for the stranger at considerable personal expense [Luke 10:25-37]. In Genesis 18, Abraham responds with hospitality to the three strangers he encounters. The ancient custom of hospitality did not permit people to "decide" whether or not the stranger was deserving of hospitality – the hospitality was expected, and it is the believer rather than the stranger who is judged for the response which is made.

The theme of hospitality is in fact a pervasive influence on Scripture and a crucial theme for the church today. I've had the pleasure of working with my friend Fred Bernhard on a book about hospitality which is titled *Widening the Welcome of Your Church* (Andrew Center, 1996). That book deals with this theme at a level of detail greater than is possible in this chapter.

We need to recognize as congregations that welcoming those who enter our doors is not simply a matter of doing something that is good for church growth or of showing friendship in the same way we do in a civic organization or at a place of business. Our Lord encourages us and challenges us to embrace the strangers who come into our midst. And if those who are strangers to the church come because they have already built a relationship with us outside of the church, then they are not strangers at all.

The Role of Friendship

George Barna, in *User Friendly Churches*, describes one of the most effective strategies for seeing that those who are invited to church end up becoming assimilated members: "The strategy called for the person who did the inviting to also provide the on-site hospitality and the post-visit debriefing . . . . This perspective of making the host responsible for follow-up is a major point of distinction for most churches that actively pursue growth" [p. 100].

Many of the problems discussed thus far in this chapter fail to present barriers when the person who invites someone to church assumes the responsibility for helping that person become incorporated into the life of the congregation. This approach happens to be excellent from a pragmatic point of view, but it is in fact simply a logical extension of the friendship around which the person was invited to church in the first place.

Studies of the way in which people become assimilated into a congregation and continue with high commitment (attendance, volunteer work, and financial support) year-after-year show that certain characteristics are most likely to be part of the church experience for those with high activity:

High Commitment People

- Find the worship services inspirational and strongly connected to daily life.

- Have their closest friendships with others who are in the congregation.

- Are strongly involved in one or more classes or small groups in the church. (The small group could be a study group, a prayer group, or an action group.)

- Feel that their involvement in the church is making a significant difference.

While those persons with the highest commitment level generally possess all four of the above characteristics, most members who are regular in attendance and involvement have at least two of the characteristics in their relationships with the congregation. From the beginning of people's contact with the church, we need to stay aware of the importance of those areas.

When we have motivated people to attend church by personally sharing our faith with them and inviting them to come, we've made significant progress in helping them feel a solid bond of friendship. That friendship especially needs to be nurtured until they have formed additional friendships, are incorporated into a class or small group, and are helped to feel they are making a difference in the church.

While friendship is the major factor causing people to become involved in the life of the church, not everyone who comes will do so because of such a bond. There will also be people who start coming because of a friendship bond only to find that the friends move to another community!

Mentors and Faith-Friends

Many congregations are placing increasing emphasis on the concept of mentors or faith-friends helping guide visitors and new members through the process of becoming assimilated into the life of the church. A mentor or faith-friend makes the well-being of a prospective member or of a new member a top priority.

It's best if the mentor or faith-friend can be the person who did the inviting; but if not, such a role can be filled by another person. The responsibilities generally accepted by a faith-friend also can be a guide to everyone seeking to help a person become involved in the church. Keep in mind, however, that the faith-friend roles are best when utilized by the person initially bringing the new member to the church. A description of faith-friend responsibilities as developed by one congregation follows on the next two pages. Some of the ideas included also relate to issues of discipleship which will be discussed more thoroughly in the next chapter.

Some Thing to Try

1. Think about how the Faith-Friend description might be better worded for your congregation.

2. Find someone who has recently joined your church and visit with that person about the overall kind of welcome which has been experienced.

A Faith–Friend

. . . . takes the initiative in making contact with the new member or prospective member assigned. Experience has shown that the best first contact is by a note and then a phone call, unless the person already knows the faith-friend. In the phone conversation, the faith-friend arranges to meet the individual or the family the following Sunday at the church or to pick that person or family up for church. Then the faith-friend arranges to share a meal after church or on another occasion.

. . . . helps the new member or prospective member get acquainted with others. Many people in our church have a busy agenda during the Sunday morning fellowship time – so busy that new people can too easily be neglected. The faith-friend prevents this from happening.

. . . . offers the new person the opportunity to become involved in a Sunday school class or another appropriate group. Call XXXXX XXXXXXX at XXX-XXXX for help identifying the right class or classes. It's also a good idea to call the teacher or coordinator for the class or group so that person can also reach out to the prospective member.

. . . . makes a special effort to be sure that the faith-friend meets others with whom there may be common bonds or interests.

. . . . takes the initiative to see that the faith-friend is linked with the right group or person in our church in terms of special interests like music, drama, or cooking.

. . . . is available to answer questions about the church and to respond to any concerns.

. . . . stands up with the faith-friend or friends at the time of membership confirmation and assists the pastor by pinning the flower to the person or persons and presenting the membership certificate.

. . . . makes a phone call just to indicate that the person was missed and to be sure everything is all right if that individual misses worship services, Sunday school class, or another regular group in which he or she has been participating.

. . . . sees that the nominating committee is aware of the interests and strengths of the friend(s).

. . . . remembers the friend(s) in prayer each day. Some may wish to invite the faith-friend to become a prayer partner, sharing in prayer for each other.

. . . . thinks about how he or she would want to be treated if new to the church, and uses that for guidance in making the best possible connections for this person or persons.

Chapter Eleven
Making New Friends
Part of the Family

Concept: Discipleship rather than "paper" membership or spiritual scalps should be our ultimate goal
as we enfold persons into the Christian community.

Emily was a single parent with two children, ages five and
eight. A retired couple who lived down the street from her had
invited the children and Emily to attend St. John's Church. She
was enthusiastic about how well-accepted she and her children
were by the church. She was aware that there weren't many
single persons her age in the congregation, but she had been so
warmly received that she wasn't really bothered.

With the exception of a few Vacation Bible School classes
she attended with friends while in elementary school, Emily had
not been involved in any congregation before joining St. John's.
The preaching there was biblically based, and the membership
classes she had attended emphasized the Bible. She definitely
wanted to increase her knowledge of Scripture, so she chose a
Sunday school class which was especially focused on Bible
study. Emily appreciated the broad age span of persons in the
class, which included a young married couple about her age,
several middle-aged persons, and some retirement-aged persons.

Emily's experiences with the Sunday school class did not,
unfortunately, remain positive. Emily kept trying to be an
enthusiastic participant, but she often felt that her questions
and her responses sounded foolish.

During one session, several references were made to the parable of the prodigal son. Emily did not remember the story and asked for an explanation of the parable. She felt like a complete idiot when she saw the looks on the faces of other class members after she asked the question.

In another session, she listened with growing concern as a class member talked about feeling so badly that persons who were baptized by a means other than immersion were going to hell. Emily had been baptized by immersion as part of joining the congregation, but she knew her brother had been baptized by sprinkling. She had a Quaker friend who didn't believe in physical baptism at all. Emily couldn't believe that all those people were going to hell, and she felt sure that she was misunderstanding the point the speaker was trying to make. When she expressed those thoughts to the class, she saw a couple of mouths literally drop open. The teacher rescued her with a diplomatic explanation but also suggested that the pastor had failed in not giving her clearer instruction in the membership preparation classes.

Emily was afraid that what she had said in class would cause the minister to get in trouble, and she felt more foolish than ever. She took her children to lunch that day at a restaurant near the church. As usual, she exchanged greetings with several people from the church who were also eating there. This Sunday, she was more conscious than ever of how many church members were eating with one another. The retired couple who had taken her out a couple of times after church had not asked her to share a meal for two or three months, and they had been busy the Saturday night she had invited them to be her guests for dinner.

As she and her children walked back to their table from the salad bar, she overheard a member of the Sunday school class talking with one other person in a booth. The words would stay with her: "Can you believe it? She didn't even understand the difference between immersion and sprinkling. How could she not understand that? I'm going to talk with the board about what we're requiring for membership. In my opinion, she should never have been allowed to join."

That was the last day Emily and her children ate at that restaurant or attended that church. She didn't understand how the congregation could have seemed so warm at first. Those feelings were further confirmed as week after week went by without anyone from the church expressing concern about her absence. The elderly couple who had first invited her moved to another part of town, and Emily had nothing more to do with the church other than throwing away the biweekly newsletters she received.

Ignored, Overlooked, Put-Down, or Shut Out

As discussed in the last chapter, there are many stages at which prospective members or new members of the congregation can feel ignored, overlooked, put down, or even shut out of the life of the church. While gaining people as new members certainly stands as a significant accomplishment, the process of making those persons truly a part of the congregation doesn't end with baptism or the repetition of membership vows. Emily's story is only one example. There are many others, including:

- Katie had been Roman Catholic all her life, but she joined an Anabaptist congregation when she got married. She had been a fairly inactive Catholic in recent years, and her husband Tom had always been a very active member in the Anabaptist church. She decided to worship with Tom because the church was so important to him. She did not want to completely give up her Roman Catholic heritage; and she didn't want to shock her parents too deeply, so she became what was called an "associate member" of the Anabaptist congregation.

  Katie became very active in the congregation and spent a year as an unofficial member of a committee. She and Tom attended a Sunday school class together. Then she discovered that there were several positions in the church which she was not permitted to hold because she was "only" an associate member. Her husband was shocked that his wife wasn't permitted to chair a committee. They didn't leave the church, but their activity level was greatly reduced.

- Roberta and Dave joined Pleasant Hill Church in large part because they were so excited by the

143

Thursday night contemporary service which was begun as an experiment about the time they started attending with the couple who had invited them. They not only became members of Pleasant Hill but also became very involved in the contemporary service with Dave playing the keyboard twice a month and Roberta putting up posters at places of business near the church to let more people know about the service. A single friend of Roberta started attending with them.

They were both shocked in a congregational meeting when several long-time members of the church complained bitterly that the new service was taking far too much of the pastor's time and that the forty-five person average attendance wasn't sufficient to justify that. Roberta, Dave, and others who were regulars at the service pointed out that it had grown from an average attendance of eighteen during its first month to the present forty-five, which seemed to them impressive. The vote was close, but the contemporary service was eliminated. Roberta and Dave found another church home as did Roberta's single friend and the couple who had invited them to Pleasant Hill.

- Ken and Vicki became involved in First Church through the friendship of a person who worked in the same company as Vicki. They had not been involved in a church for years, and Ken had almost stopped believing in God until coming into contact with this congregation. Ken's revitalized faith was so central to his life that he was responsible for bringing six new people into the church's membership during the first year he and Vicki were there. When a friend of Ken's was sent to prison, Ken started visiting him every week. He was overwhelmed to discover how few good programs existed to help people who served time get a second start on life when released.

Ken felt called to do something about the need and began working to establish a support group for ex-offenders at First Church. His efforts met a solid wall of resistance from people who argued that having ex-offenders in the church building could pose a danger. In spite of what Ken thought was impressive statistical evidence that the kind of ex-offender who joined a church sponsored support group was not a dangerous person, he was unable to win approval for the support group. People maintained that even nonviolent ex-offenders might steal from the church or destroy property. As Ken and Vicki visited with people who had been in the church for years, they began to recognize that the problem was not so much the target group for the ministry (ex-offenders) as the mere fact that it was a new program. A couple of sympathetic older members told Ken that it would take him two or three years to get any new program approved unless it came from the denomination, in which case it might take longer!

3,000 to Assimilate

How do we truly make the new friends we bring to church or meet at church part of the Christian community? How do we assimilate them in such a way that they remain involved in the church and excited about that involvement? How do we help them become disciples, active followers of Jesus Christ? The Bible offers some helpful perspective.

Acts 2:14-47 describes an occasion of fantastic growth in the early church. Moved by Peter's eloquent address to them and by the Holy Spirit's presence, three thousand people were added to the Christian community at one time [verse 41]. That was, in fact, only one phase of a time of continuing growth for the church. We learn in verse forty-four that "day by day the Lord added to their number those who were being saved."

Many of our churches have problems assimilating a relatively small number of people into the life of the congregation. What would it be like to receive three thousand? In some respects, of course, it can be easier to assimilate a large number of persons because their very mass forces change on the congregation; but the task would have been enormous. In studying the second chapter of Acts, we learn that the early church did several things

145

to help assimilate new members and enable those persons to grow in their discipleship:

• **They taught.** Most of the new converts would have known little about the life and teachings of Jesus. The New Testament Scriptures as they exist for us today, in fact, were not available to these early Christians. The apostles had to teach new Christians what they needed to know about Jesus Christ.

If you are successful in reaching persons who have not grown up in the church or who have not been involved in the church for a substantial period of time, teaching will be one of the most important aspects of helping them become part of the Christian community. While membership preparation classes can and should cover many areas, it's impossible for them to cover everything. Neither Emily nor the pastor is necessarily to blame for her not having grasped every aspect of her church's view of baptism.

As we saw in Emily's situation, members of the congregation need to be helped to have sensitivity to the fact that new members may not be familiar with things that long-term members take for granted. The people in Emily's class almost certainly did not mean to be rude to her or to make her feel put-down. They were not accustomed to dealing with a person who had grown up with relatively little exposure to the Bible or to the life of a congregation. They did not think about how their responses to Emily would make her feel. Study of a book like *Sharing Living Water* is one effective way to increase the awareness of long-time members of the needs of new members.

• **They prayed and shared communion.** They prayed for the new converts and also taught them to pray. As discussed in the third chapter of this book, the devotional life is absolutely crucial to Christian growth. Those who are already members and those who are new members are alike in needing to continually deepen their personal relationships with Christ. Prayer needs to permeate our individual lives and also the life of the congregation. Communion can play an important role in helping us deepen our faith and live more fully as disciples.

• **They spent time together.** The new members had become part of a spiritual family and loved spending time together. Becoming a Christian brings not only a new relationship with God through Christ but also new relationships with others. While people can gain a sense of community in large worship services, most people form their strongest relationships in smaller groupings of the congregation: classes, social groups, work groups, and even boards and committees of the church. Both in groups established for the purpose of helping people become better acquainted and in groups which have task-oriented agenda, it remains important for us to provide opportunities to help people draw closer to one another.

Informal social opportunities are also part of that process. While Emily and her children had shared a couple of meals with the people who initially invited them to the church, they had not been invited to share a meal or a social time with others in recent months. Most of our congregations need to seek opportunities to help newer and long-time members socialize informally. Variations on a program sometimes called "Dinner for Eight" have been a significant help in many congregations. A host family invites between six and ten people to come share a meal and visit with one another. The mix of people intentionally includes relatively new members and those who have been part of the congregation for many years.

• **They shared possessions.** Wanting to be sure every person had enough, the members of the early church shared what they had with one another: "All who believed were together and had all things in common; they would sell their possessions and goods and distribute the proceeds to all, as any had need" [Acts 2:44-45]. This is not the model around which our contemporary congregations have been built!

While new members in most of our churches are not likely to need food or clothing, this passage reminds us that we should take seriously the needs of one another within the Christian community. The insights of chapter six on the various kinds of need which people experience should apply to those inside the church as readily as to those outside the church. Churches often fail to consider the possibility that there may be people in the congregation with physical needs. This can be especially true for elderly persons who are often living on fixed incomes.

Periods of unemployment sometimes keep people away from the church. We need to be sensitive to such concerns, not only for new members but also for long-time members. Many churches have some kind of social action fund which is available to provide short-term help to persons in the Christian community who are having difficulty meeting their physical needs.

- **They made more disciples.** Those who joined the early church also reached out to others in love and service. Often the newest members of a congregation are the most enthusiastic at sharing their faith with others and drawing others into the life of the church. Ken certainly displayed that at First Church in the example shared earlier in this chapter.

Become a Permission-Giving Church

Established churches in the Roman Catholic, Protestant, and Anabaptist traditions have almost all devoted considerable energy to the control of what happens in congregational life. That has created decision-making structures which are extremely slow in many churches and has also made resistance to change a permanent part of the ethos of those congregations. Bill Easum, in his insightful book *Sacred Cows Make Gourmet Burgers*, warns [p.9] that:

> *Established churches must either cease worshiping the god of control, or they perish!*

Control is the sacred cow of established churches. The new member problems shared at the beginning of this chapter dealt in large part with issues of control:

- Katie and Tom became disillusioned with their church primarily because of the refusal to let an "associate member" like Katie be the chairperson of a board or committee. The church held to that position in spite of the fact that Tom had grown up in the church and that he and Katie together were two of the most active and supportive participants in congregational life. The desire to control which persons are permitted to hold certain responsibilities was given greater weight than Katie's obvious skills and commitment to the church. Younger people, especially if they did not grow up in the church, are not likely to be as concerned over membership issues as older members. Some churches, especially in western states and provinces, have young adult participants who simply do not care about formal organizational membership enough to bother joining, though they may be quite active.

- Roberta and Dave became disillusioned with the inability of the congregation as a whole to be supportive of a more contemporary approach to worship. There was in fact no good reason to shut down the contemporary service other than a generalized anxiety that the pastor was devoting too much time to the service. Other issues at work may have included whether or not the new people coming for the contemporary service were personally known to members of the congregation who attended the regular Sunday services.

- Ken and Vicki discovered that the church was very slow to change and also very protective of its physical property. Too many people were not able to catch a glimpse of Ken's vision for the support group.

Most of our churches need to become more permission-giving instead of controlling. When faced with a new idea, the normal response should be "Why not?" If there is no compelling reason not to try something and if at least some members are supportive of the proposal, the church should move ahead. There can be wisdom in referring to some new efforts as experimental so that it's possible to graciously bring them to an end if they are not achieving the desired result. A new effort like a separate contemporary service, however, may require substantial time to show clear numerical results.

Congregations which want to enfold new people into the Christian family need to be cautious in making assumptions about what people know from the past and about how things should be run in the present and future. For example:

149

• **New members and prospective members shouldn't be expected to have vast knowledge of the Scriptures and of the traditions of the church.** Classes and study opportunities are important for the entire congregation as people seek to grow in discipleship, but such opportunities can be especially empowering for those who are new to the church. As already discussed, long-time members of the congregation need help in better understanding people like Emily who did not grow up in the church. Churches also need to provide adequate orientation for persons who accept responsibilities such as ushering, teaching, or serving on a board or committee. It's easy for churches who have not assimilated many new members in recent years to inaccurately assume that "everyone knows what to do" in a given position. Of course the same orientation will likely be of help to anyone in a new volunteer position.

• **The church shouldn't assume that new members and constituents will automatically get to know others in the congregation.** Several strategies can help new people develop relationships in the church:

- The use of faith-friends or mentors continuing through the first year of membership.
- The effective involvement of people in small groups.
- The use of strategies such as "Dinners for Eight," which was discussed earlier in this chapter.
- The provision of training for all members of the congregation, to help them more comfortably reach out to new people.

• **Churches need to drop the concept that one must belong to a congregation for five to ten years in order to hold certain positions of leadership.** With rapid mobility affecting so many people, congregations need to learn how to involve new members far more quickly than in the past. It's important, of course, not to push people into experiences which they aren't yet ready to tackle; but most established churches err in the direction of an unwillingness to put newer members into significant positions of leadership.

• **Congregations need to be careful about too quickly assuming what kinds of volunteer work are best for new members.** There is a tendency for newer members to be slotted into particular positions such as teaching in the Sunday school or singing in the choir but to be excluded from others, such as serving on the finance commission, the property committee, or the official board of the church. A new member who works as a certified public accountant may appreciate the change of pace that comes with teaching an elementary Sunday school class, but that person might also feel that the finance commission is a better place to serve in terms of utilizing his or her gifts.

• **Churches can also be too quick to assume that something can't be done because it has not been possible in the past.** For example, many congregations do not feel they have sufficient volunteers, or in some cases financial resources, to accomplish the following:

- Provide child care at all church classes and meetings.
- Develop a separate contemporary worship service or have more contemporary worship as part of the regular service.
- Start a single parents' ministry.
- Build a gym to enhance the youth program.

Rather than too quickly assuming that such things can't be accomplished, church leadership should look at the possibilities as well as the problems. Those persons with a strong interest in a given project should be encouraged to creatively explore how it can be accomplished. The energy of new people may be the catalyst to make it possible!

• **Congregations need to focus more on action groups or ministry teams than on elaborate decision-making structures.** An action group or ministry team could be the ideal way to study and implement any one of the new ideas listed in the previous section (child care, a contemporary service, . . .). Such teams come together to carry out a particular assignment and generally work with a great deal of autonomy, which makes rapid progress possible.

The autonomy which such groups are often given can present the appearance of group members being "out of control" or "not accountable" for their actions. Obviously a proposal for something like the construction of a gymnasium eventually needs to come to a board or a congregational meeting (depending on the organizational structure of your church); but not every new idea needs to be sanctioned at the highest level in the church. The issue very often is not that the ministry team is out of control but rather that some members of the congregation are not themselves *in control.* When long-time members of the congregation are helped to become acquainted with newer members, trust can be developed which will facilitate a more open attitude toward innovation.

• **We should recognize that consensus can be a wise way to make some major decisions but that it isn't the only approach.** A permission-giving church recognizes that many decisions can be made by a small group which then moves ahead. Easum warns: "Established churches are so addicted to group process and consensus building they don't encourage individuals to exercise their God-given gifts on behalf of the body of Christ" [p. 62].

• **Increasingly the greatest energy for growth and outreach comes in churches which encourage true "bottom up" programming.** Established congregations are accustomed to a model in which new programming comes from the denominational offices or grows out of a brainstorming or planning session of the major governing board of the church. While some good programming and strategy obviously emerges from these initiatives, more emphasis needs to be placed on the input and involvement of the whole congregation. Permission-giving churches encourage people with creative ideas to form action teams, involve others in the process, and work toward implementation.

Congregational surveys for feedback on the quality of the church's life and program become valuable planning tools for leaders concerned with quality and with obtaining the input of everyone who is part of the church family. For more perspective on becoming a permission-giving congregation and on working for change and quality in the church, we especially recommend:

> *Change and the Established Congregation* by Paul
> Mundey (Andrew Center Resources)
> *Creating Quality in Ministry* by Steve Clapp and
> Cindy Hollenberg Snider (Andrew Center Resources)
> *Sacred Cows Make Gourmet Burgers* by Bill Easum
> (Abingdon)

Look at the Role of Small Groups

Chapter ten discussed the characteristics most often present in persons who have high levels of commitment to the church. Strong small group life in the congregation can help people experience or gain three of those four characteristics:

High Commitment People

- Find the worship services inspirational and strongly connected to daily life.

- Have their closest friendships with others who are in the congregation.

- Are strongly involved in one or more classes or small groups in the church. (The small group could be a study group, a prayer group, or an action group.)

- Feel that their involvement in the church is making a significant difference.

While small group life generally incorporates prayer and some other features of worship, participation in a small group will not necessarily help a person find the congregational worship services meaningful and inspirational. Involvement in a small group itself, however, meets one of the four characteristics. That involvement is also likely to result in two other characteristics: the formation of closer friendships and people feeling their involvement in the church makes a difference – through what they contribute to the small group life and at times through what the small group and its members contribute to the church.

There are two general structures for small group life in the congregation. While they are not mutually exclusive, most churches tend to emphasize one approach or the other.

The first approach focuses on the creation of small groups for everyone in the church. When the whole church (aside from the chronically inactive who participate in virtually nothing) becomes involved in these groups, they are often referred to as cell groups and may become the major focus for congregational life. People in these groups:

- Pray together.
- Study together.
- Nurture and strengthen group life.
- Minister to one another in times of illness and crisis.
- Reach out to friends of group members and seek to involve them in the small group and the church.
- Divide when necessary because the group has grown too large.

New members immediately become involved in a cell group and thus can be integrated very quickly into congregational life because they become part of an intimate fellowship which cares for them and involves them in caring for others. Many resources are available on cell ministry and on nurturing small group life. Bill Easum's book *Dancing with Dinosaurs* (Abingdon) shares an insightful look at the ways cell groups function and at their impact on a congregation. Herb Miller's book *Connecting with God* (Abingdon) is an outstanding resource on nurturing the spiritual life in the church and talks about the role of "loving groups" in the lives of individuals and the church.

The second approach focuses on nurturing small group life through a wide variety of classes and groups. While some of these groups may be more task-centered than a cell group would be, the nurturing of group life and encouraging group members to be supportive of one another are considered part of the purpose of every class, small group, board, and committee in the congregation. The types of groups which can function in this way include:

- Sunday school classes
- Prayer groups
- Bible study groups
- Spiritual growth groups
- Youth groups
- Men's groups
- Women's groups

- Support groups for people in various life
  situations such as:
  - Single Parents
  - Empty Cradle (parents who have lost an
    infant or young child)
  - Parents of Teenagers
  - Alcoholics Anonymous
  - Sugarbusters (diabetics)
  - Better Health Group (persons seeking to
    lose weight and improve their overall health)
  - Teen Empowerment (a group for teens who
    are having trouble with the law or with other
    authority figures)
- Boards and committees
- Task forces and mission groups
- Musical groups
- Senior citizen/retirement groups

Such a congregation stays continually alert for the need to form new small groups to involve new people or to respond to the ideas and concerns of people. When a person joins the congregation (if not before), the church sees that the individual becomes involved in at least one small group opportunity. The way each group functions will depend on its unique purpose and on the needs of those who participate in the group. The flow for a group meeting might be something like this:

1. An opening prayer.
2. Sharing of joys and concerns from group members.
3. Focus on the agenda for the meeting (the study
   topic for a class; the business agenda for a board
   or committee; . . .).
4. A closing time to identify any issues or problems
   of group members which were not shared during
   the joys and concerns.
5. An open prayer time in which people pray as moved
   for one another, the group, the church, and the
   world.

One strategy for helping so many different groups include the nurturing of one another as a regular part of their time together is to have an annual retreat for leaders or representatives from all the groups. The retreat can be a time to talk together about the importance of small group life in the church and about what can be done to nurture that group life in the many different settings.

Responding Personally

The focus of this chapter has been on the role of the congregation as a whole in helping new members become a part of the church family and grow in discipleship. The very best way to keep a new member from being left out, of course, is for a faith-friend or mentor (as described in the tenth chapter) to stay in close contact for at least the first year of membership. The faith-friend or mentor can intervene if the new member is not getting involved in the group life of the congregation or is not satisfied with a group in which he or she has been participating.

If the congregation as a whole does not recognize the importance of embracing new members and of being open to change and innovation in the life of the church, then the best efforts of a faith-friend or mentor may not be sufficient. Roberta and Dave, whose situation was described near the beginning of this chapter, dropped out in spite of continued concern from the couple who had invited them to the church. In fact that couple went with them to a new congregation! A faith-friend or mentor program can be of great value, but it doesn't lower the importance of the congregation as a whole gaining deeper appreciation for new members and seeking to encourage a diversity of ministries by both new and long-time members of the church.

If a new member (or any member for that matter!) breaks a pattern of regular attendance at worship, Sunday school, or a small group, it is crucial for the church to reach out to that person without delay. Strategies for monitoring attendance and responding to breaks in attendance are covered in more detail in Steve Clapp's book *Overcoming Barriers to Church Growth* and in Steve Clapp and Jerry O. Cook's book *Reaching Out Through Christian Education* (both are Andrew Center publications).

Some Things to Try

1.   If you are currently involved in a class or a small group in your church (or in another setting if that group is open to new members), complete the "Are We Open or Closed Around Here?" exercise which follows this chapter. You may want to visit about your responses with another person who is in the group.

2.   If you do not belong to a church, try visiting one which you've heard others discuss in positive terms. Identify the opportunities in that church which can help new persons become part of the Christian community and grow in discipleship. If you are not satisfied with what you find in the congregation, talk to the pastor and other church leaders about your observations!

3.   If you already belong to a church, find out if any persons who have joined your congregation in the past three years have become inactive. Visit one or more of them to find out why they dropped out. You may wish to share what you learn with the pastor and other church leaders.

Are We Open or Closed Around Here?

*How easy or difficult is it for new people to get inside your group –
to really start belonging? Indicate the strength of your agreement
with each of the following statements by placing an **X** at the
appropriate spot on the line.*

1. Everyone in the group feels included in discussions and
   activities.

   Strongly Disagree   Strongly Agree

2. Several people (who have not moved out of the community)
   have stopped attending the group over the last year.

   Strongly Disagree   Strongly Agree

3. When a new person attends our group for the first time,
   the rest of us do a good job welcoming that person and
   reaching out to that person at times in addition to the
   group meetings.

   Strongly Disagree   Strongly Agree

4. The group consistently shows genuine concern about
   all group members including those who have just started
   coming.

   Strongly Disagree   Strongly Agree

5. If a person stops coming to the group, we have a
   clear procedure for reaching out to that person.

   Strongly Disagree   Strongly Agree

Chapter Twelve
Expanding the Friendship Circle

Concept: Recognizing that Christ's definition of "neighbor" is broader than our own, we should be at work expanding our circle of friends and reaching out to a world in need.

During my high school years, Star Trek was one of my favorite television programs. The show represented what at that time was high quality science fiction, but it also dealt with a range of social issues. The demographics of the spaceship Enterprise's bridge conveyed a more inclusive view of humankind than I saw portrayed on any other television series. The officers included a North American captain, an African communications officer, an Asian pilot, a Russian pilot, and a science officer from the planet Vulcan.

While the majority on the crew were white, the racial diversity went beyond tokenism; and many episodes of the series focused on appreciation for persons from different cultures. While the original Star Trek series has been consigned to the realm of reruns on television and the main characters reappear only in an occasional motion picture, two newer television series were developed under the Star Trek umbrella: the Next Generation and Deep Space Nine. Both of these series have increased the diversity of the cast with people from many different solar systems.

If you are not a science fiction fan and immediately channel-hop when spaceships flash across the television screen, then you may not have visual images to accompany the preceding paragraphs. Through the years in North America, science fiction has been one of the ways that attitudes toward the unfamiliar have been expressed. Many of the science fiction movies of the 1940s and 1950s, for example, portrayed those from other planets as hostile and dangerous, reflective of the protective attitudes of the time. The civil rights movement which gained momentum in the sixties, the shrinking of our world through technology, and the radical changes taking place all over our planet have pushed us to somewhat greater acceptance of diversity. The fact that the lead parts in most science fiction still go to white males, of course, shows that we still have far to go!

We also have far to go in the typical North American congregation, in which we've not done particularly well with outreach to those who differ significantly from the majority of the church membership. Glide Memorial United Methodist Church in San Francisco stands as one of the significant exceptions. The senior pastor of that congregation, Cecil Williams, has intentionally encouraged outreach to and acceptance of people from all walks of life. While pleased with much that he has accomplished at Glide, Williams remains deeply concerned about church life:

> *It seems to me that Sunday morning is still the most*
> *segregated hour in America. That really does speak*
> *against what the church should be doing. I'd like to*
> *have an exodus occur where the churches began to*
> *move to a real critical point in their lives where they*
> *will become more inclusive and stop worrying about*
> *a person's sexual identity or a person's color, a*
> *person's class or whatever. We've got to move beyond*
> *that.*

Williams himself has done more than just talk about making the church inclusive. When he came to Glide over thirty years ago, he "invited in the destitute from the strip-clubs, X-rated movie theaters, and flop houses that surrounded Glide. Within a month, he was involved in a battle to protect prostitutes from police brutality . . . . Eventually, he began offering classes to help people kick drug and alcohol habits." Glide Church today has a huge congregation truly including persons from all sorts of economic, ethnic, and occupational backgrounds. The church operates numerous outreach programs and self-help classes and has become a major center for free meals for the poor. [The material on Cecil Williams and Glide Church comes in part from the

Sat., Jan. 27, 1996, *Journal Gazette* article on page 1C: *Minister Preaches Inte-gration* by Karyn Hunt of Associated Press.]

When most of our congregations think of outreach, they are not envisioning persons of different racial backgrounds and certainly not persons who have been patronizing or operating strip-clubs or flop houses! The truth of the matter is that the majority of congregations in North America have experienced difficulty accepting diversity along far less radical lines:

- Most congregations have not been able to successfully embrace any significant range of economic diversity. In the typical community, there are some congregations which are composed primarily of low-income house-holds, the majority which are essentially middle-income, and a few which are high-income. Many churches which claim to have people of all economic levels are, in fact, almost exclusively middle-income, with a few persons going through temporarily difficult times of unemployment and perhaps one high-income house-hold.

- Racial diversity obviously poses a significant challenge to congregations, but there are other kinds of ethnic diversity which are also difficult. Several Protestant and Anabaptist congregations have historically been so identified with a particular European ancestry, such as German or Swiss, that it is difficult for them to as quickly embrace persons of other backgrounds. When persons in these congregations meet a visitor, their first line of conversation is likely to be an effort to discover whether or not they know someone who knows the visitor. To the visitor, this sounds like a litmus test for acceptance.

- While most congregations have grown more accepting of members who have been divorced, a great many still find it difficult to immediately embrace persons who are single parents. This becomes especially hard if the single parent has never been married but has chosen to raise a child. All of our communities, how-ever, have large numbers of single parents who are open to church involvement, if the congregation can truly welcome them.

161

- Many congregations which are composed largely of older members find it awkward to fully embrace younger people who come with different opinions on how the church should do its work. Some of these differences were discussed in the previous chapter on assimilating people into the life of the congregation.

The word "diversity" has taken on some particular political connotations with many persons in North America. The use of the word in this chapter does not refer to any political agenda but rather to the reality of the diversity in the body of Christ and of the mission statement which Jesus gave those of us who call ourselves Christians:

> *Go into all the world and proclaim the good news to the whole creation.*
> **Mark 16:14**

A Biblical Look at the Circle of Friendship

Members of Glide Church were distressed by the presence of the strip-clubs, X-rated movie theaters, and flop houses around the church. Many of them were understandably shocked when Williams began reaching out to the people in those establishments, people the church had learned to regard with suspicion and even fear. Yet Williams is not the first person to reach out to those other religious leaders wished to avoid. Our Lord repeatedly offended the religious authorities by his concern for outsiders.

Luke 19:1-10 describes an incident which occurred when Jesus passed through the town of Jericho on his way to Jerusalem. The crowd gathered to see Jesus had no doubt heard many stories about his healings, his miracles, and his confrontations with Jewish leaders.

Today, as was the case then, Jesus presents a challenge for those who approach primarily out of curiosity or out of a desire to see what can be personally gained by association with him. Such persons may seek his justification and help for their causes, their prejudices, and their lifestyles. They are not searching for a life-changing encounter which will bring them into conflict with the world and its ways.

Zacchaeus had reached the top of his profession as a tax collector and was a wealthy man as a result. Tax collectors were so hated, however, that Zacchaeus probably had few friends. He may have been filled with loneliness, emptiness, and guilt. Whatever the motivation, Zacchaeus wanted to see Jesus so much that he climbed a sycamore tree.

Jesus had sensitivity and compassion for those rejected by others. He was able to look above the crowd and see this small man, hanging in the top of a sycamore tree, desperate to catch a glimpse of him. Unconcerned with what the crowd thought of his actions, Jesus invited himself to Zacchaeus' house. The crowd was not happy: "All who saw it began to grumble and said, 'He has gone to be the guest of one who is a sinner'" [v. 19:7].

Our Lord did not approach Zacchaeus ready to immediately condemn him for his sins. Jesus spoke to him with compassion, acceptance, and graciousness, explaining his actions in these words: "For the Son of Man came to seek out and save the lost" [v. 19:10]. The acceptance of Jesus transformed the life of Zacchaeus, who pledged to give half his possessions to the poor and pay back anyone he had defrauded four-fold. This went far beyond what he was expected by law to repay [see Leviticus 6:5; Numbers 5:7].

The New Testament contains numerous examples of acceptance being shown for those who live on the margins of society and of the clear intention that the good news of Christ is to be shared, without qualification, with all people. For example:

Matthew 28:16-20. *Go therefore and make disciples of all nations, baptizing them in the name of the Father and of the Son and of the Holy Spirit, and teaching them to obey everything that I have commanded you. And remember, I am with you always, to the end of the age* [v.19-20]. These words of the Great Commission have challenged Christians through the centuries, and they continue to challenge us today. How can we learn to reach out to all people, including those who are opposed to much that we do and those who make us uncomfortable?

Luke 10:25-37. *You shall love the Lord your God with all your heart, and with all your soul, and with all your strength, and with all your mind; and your neighbor as yourself* [v.27]. In response to that statement from Jesus, a lawyer asked him: *And who is my neighbor?* [v.29]. Jesus answered his question by telling the Parable of the Good Samaritan. Our neighbors are all those with whom we come in contact, all those who are in need. Jesus does not permit us to exclude certain persons as unworthy or objectionable.

Luke 14:12-24. *But when you give a banquet, invite the poor, the crippled, the lame, and the blind. And you will be blessed, because they cannot repay you, for you will be repaid at the resurrection of the righteous* [v.13-14]. Those verses are followed by what has become known as the Parable of the Great Dinner. When those who had been invited to the banquet did not come, a broader invitation was extended: *Go out at once into the streets and lanes of the town and bring in the poor, the crippled, the blind, and the lame* [v. 21b].

John 8:1-11. *Let anyone among you who is without sin be the first to throw a stone at her* [v.7]. Jesus spoke these words to protect a woman who had been caught in the act of adultery. He had no interest in condemning her or in supporting those who condemned her.

Acts 1:6-8. *You will receive power when the Holy Spirit has come upon you; and you will be my witnesses in Jerusalem, in all Judea and Samaria, and to the ends of the earth* [v.8]. There is truly no limit on the scope of persons with whom we are urged to share the good news of Jesus Christ.

Adding to the Friendship Circle

What can you and I do as individuals and through our congregations to expand the circle of friendship? We can choose from a wide range of strategies. Most of us should not attempt to be too ambitious at first. If your church has difficulty simply enabling the younger adult children of present members to feel welcome and accepted, you are probably not ready as a congregation to reach out to a neighbor-hood of a different race than your own. If you find it awkward to talk about the church or the faith with your neighbor three doors down the street, you may not be ready to start visiting with a prison inmate.

On the other hand, sometimes a radical change in our outreach efforts will prove easier to accomplish than gradual change. You need to decide what is right for you as an individual and what you want to propose to your congregation. Here are a few ideas to consider:

- Do you know someone who takes care of a severely
  disabled child or adult? Find out how you could be
  of help to that individual and to the disabled person.
  Find out what barriers, if any, keep the disabled
  person from sharing in the life of a congregation.
  The barriers could be something like a ramp but may
  also be the perceived attitudes of people in the church.
  Enlist the help of others in providing a ramp and in
  changing attitudes if needed.

- Do you find that your church is one of those in which
  visitors may have difficulty feeling welcome if they do
  not share a common European ancestry? If that's the
  case, accept as a personal mission working to change
  those attitudes in your church. Remember that the
  members of the church are probably not wanting to
  exclude others, but they probably are not aware of
  how their attitudes affect the ability of the church to
  be a truly welcoming community.

- Do you find that you have almost no friends who are
  not already members of a church? Depending on
  which set of survey data one wishes to believe and

the part of the country in which you live, between thirty and fifty percent of the population consists of persons who are not members of a local church. The percentage who belong but are not active is, of course, higher! Think about what keeps you from developing friendships with unchurched persons. Do some of those you know use language which offends you? Do you come across in a judgmental way which makes them want to avoid you? Whatever the blocks, work on expanding your own circle of friends by developing relationships with one or more persons who are not part of the life of any church.

- Do you know someone who has AIDS or who is involved in a task force or ministry doing work about AIDS? Find an opportunity to develop a friendship with someone who has AIDS, or join an organization which offers support to persons with AIDS or education to the public about AIDS. You will find opportunities to extend the love of Christ, and you may find opportunities to recommend initiatives which would help your church reach out to persons with AIDS. If you find this suggestion distasteful, pass right on by – but consider the possibility that you need to learn more about AIDS in order to be less frightened and in order to understand something affecting so many in society. What would Jesus do?

- Do you have a friendship with someone of another race? In particular, if you are black, do you have a white friend? If you are white, do you have a black friend? Note that the question here is about friendship, not simply about being acquainted with someone. Depending on your own race and on where you live, the ethnic background you should be thinking about could be Hispanic, Korean, Chinese, Vietnamese, Native American, or something else. Unless you live in a very homogeneous rural community, there are very likely opportunities to form such a friendship. If no such opportunities are available to you, then consider joining an organization or doing some kind of volunteer work which would bring you into relationships with people of another race. Developing such a relationship into a true

friendship will enrich your life and may also begin
to affect your view of the church.

- If your church is located in a neighborhood which
  has gone through so much transition that many of
  the persons living near the church are of a different
  racial or economic background than those who are
  members of the church, seek ways for your church
  to reach out to the neighborhood. This could mean
  hiring a person of another race to be on the church
  staff, even if that is initially a part-time position.
  You may want to visit on a door-to-door basis. You
  may want to start simply by developing a personal
  relationship with someone of a different racial or
  economic background in the neighborhood.

- Do you know a person who has been sentenced to
  a term in jail or prison? If not, there may well
  be a community organization which seeks to put
  persons in touch with inmates who want contact
  with the outside world. Start corresponding with
  a prisoner. Don't preach, don't ask questions about
  the crime, and don't assume the incarcerated person
  lacks religious faith. Be accepting, ask about life in
  prison or jail, and seek to build a relationship. If
  you develop a friendship by correspondence, you
  may want to visit the person in prison or jail. Your
  outreach could change the life of the individual and
  could also result in that person's becoming involved
  in the life of your church when released.

- Do you know a young person who has a track
  record of getting in trouble at school or with law
  enforcement authorities? If not, there are probably
  organizations in your community seeking to help
  such young people. Find one young person with
  whom you can build a relationship. Practice the
  kind of listening and caring skills described in
  earlier chapters of this book. Through your involvement with that young person, you may be able to
  bring about a transformation in his or her life and
  eventually encourage outreach to youth by others
  in your congregation.

- Do you know a teenage unwed mother or the parents of one? Virtually every community in the United States has teenage girls who are not married but who are taking care of a child. Put aside any judgmental feelings you may have about the fact that the young person became pregnant or the fact that the infant was kept rather than released for adoption. (Remember that if the teenager had chosen to have an abortion, you would not even know there had been a pregnancy.) Build a relationship with such a person. You will have a unique opportunity to make a difference in the life of the teenager and also in the life of the teenager's child. If you are successful in getting the young person to attend church activities with you, you will probably need to run some interference so that others do not unthinkingly say things which will sound judgmental to the young person. As you develop the relationship with the teenager, you will almost certainly discover that judgment is not what is needed – acceptance and love in Christ will bring far better results. You may be able to initiate a church-wide effort to reach out to young people in similar situations.

- Don't forget that people on the upper end of the economic ladder can be just as hungry for true friendship as those at the bottom of the ladder. Join a club or organization which will involve you in interaction with the people who think of themselves as "movers and shakers" in the community. Seek opportunities to build relationships with persons in that group who are not involved in the life of a local church.

- Is there a university or college in your community? What kinds of ministries are being offered to the students? Many commuter campuses are not served with regularity by any organized ministry. Investigate the opportunities available to individuals and congregations to become involved with an existing ministry or to initiate one.

- Are there situations in your community in which physical, economic, or social needs are responded to by community agencies, but spiritual needs go unmet? For example, many mental health centers are prohibited from dealing with spiritual issues because of federal funding. While they may do a fine job dealing with psychological and social issues, they need assistance in helping with the spiritual components of recovery. Discover what opportunities for that kind of outreach may exist.

A Personal Reflection on Outreach

Opportunities for significant outreach ministries by the congregation can result from individuals responding to the identified needs of others. Three years ago, I was asked to visit in the county jail with a relative of a church family. After several weeks of regular visits, he told me there were other inmates in his cell block who wanted to talk with a pastor. I began visiting with more people, and then jail officials asked me to serve communion to inmates during Holy Week.

At this point, I knew that the ministry was growing beyond the limitations of my time and energy and that more people needed to be involved. Both from the pulpit and in the church newsletter, I asked members to pray for God's discernment as to whether or not our church should be pursuing this ministry. People kept affirming my involvement and said they would like to be part of it.

Before expanding the ministry, the church took two important steps. First, we spoke with jail officials about what was possible. Second, we contacted Prison Fellowship which agreed to provide training for interested persons in our church. Those who received instruction formed a Jail Ministry Team to plan and implement outreach programs to prisoners and their families. The congregation's ministry in this area had four components:

1. I began offering a weekly worship service at the county jail.

2. Our lay people became willing to work with the families of inmates to help meet their needs.

3. We became involved in a Prison Fellowship program

called Angel Tree in which we bought Christmas presents for the children of inmates in our area.

4. We committed ourselves to helping inmates with employment, housing, and personal and family issues upon their release. As part of this, we strongly encouraged them to attend our church so they could be nurtured by the entire faith community.

Since our initial ministry began, we have added two other components. First, a member of our congregation, who is a recovering alcoholic, has begun conducting 12-step meetings at the county jail. Second, we have maintained our contact with Prison Fellowship so that we have continuing training opportunities for new persons wanting to help and renewal experiences for those already involved. This experience has been enriching for all of us who have been involved, and our church has added families as a direct result of the outreach effort.

Two cautions need to be shared concerning outreach ministries. First, people who worship with us often have needs as significant as any in the community. Christians are not immune to personal and social problems. Child abuse, alcoholism, mental illness, prison families, and dysfunctional families all exist within our congregations. We should remain sensitive to the importance of identifying and dealing with the special needs of our own people. Out of that ministry, we will discover resources and opportunities for outreach to the larger community. The jail and prison ministry just described grew out of one person's response to a request from one family. We must not, however, focus only on the needs of people already in the church; or we will never get around to outreach!

Second, we need to enter these outreach programs with a spirit of mutuality and humility. We may know some things about faith and about the transformational power of Jesus Christ because of our religious upbringing or our spiritual maturity. Those we seek to help, nevertheless, have many things to teach us. Some have survived life crises we cannot even imagine. Others have much to teach us about overcoming seemingly impossible obstacles and maintaining faith in the face of adversity. They will often be our best resources in building and expanding our outreach efforts.

Some Things to Try

1. Go back to the list of suggestions under "Adding to the Friendship Circle" (page 165 and following). Identify one specific idea which looks realistic for you as an individual or for the congregation of which you are a part. Develop a strategy for reaching out in that way.

2. Involve your congregation's leadership in a careful assessment of the interests and needs in your congregation and of the opportunities for ministry which exist in the community. The Andrew Center's Congregational Profile offers an excellent process for that kind of study. For more information, contact The Andrew Center at 1-800-774-3360.

☞ *Look again* at an overview of the *faith–sharing process suggested in this book.*

We can comfortably relate our faith in Christ to others and invite others into the life of the church through a process of:
- Forming genuine friendships.
- Listening to the needs of our friends and learning to ask deeper questions.
- Caring for our friends and showing that care in words and actions.
- Telling in our own words how Christ and the church have made a difference in our lives, building not so much on our strength or wisdom as on our weakness.
- Inviting others into the life of the congregation.
- Helping those who join the church become fully incorporated into the body of Christ.
- Recognizing that it is Christ who saves and that we must respect where others are in openness to Christ and the church.

You've finished the book. If you've not already begun to reach out to others, now is the time to start. If you're not already on The Andrew Center's mailing list, the next page tells you how to do that. They'll be glad to keep you posted on new resources for evangelism and church growth.

About *The Andrew Center*

The mission of The Andrew Center is to multiply the number of persons turning to Jesus Christ by multiplying the number of leaders and congregations spiritually alive and evangelistically effective.

The Andrew Center was started with the initiative and financing of the Church of the Brethren, one of the oldest denominations in North America; but the *Center* exists to serve persons of all denominational backgrounds. The following denominations are in a partnership relation with *The Andrew Center:* The Brethren Church (Ashland, Ohio), the General Conference Mennonite Church, and the Mennonite Church. Persons from over twenty different denominational traditions (including Baptists, Disciples of Christ, Episcopalians, Lutherans, Presbyterians, and United Methodists) work with us.

We seek to enable leaders and congregations by:

- **Resourcing** with tested materials, ideas, and services to meet the needs of the local church.

- **Consulting** in congregational revitalization, faith–sharing and church growth, spiritual gift discovery, and other areas of congregational concern.

- **Training** at locations around the United States and Canada on practical topics such as reaching young families, handling change in the church, and sharing the faith with others.

- **Networking** people together for mutual support and idea exchange.

An **Action Guide and Catalog** of our products and services can be obtained at no charge. Many congregations elect to partner with us by becoming members of the *Center*. Membership provides special benefits to the leaders or congregation joining and also furthers the *Center*'s research and development. For more information, call or write:

The Andrew Center
1451 Dundee Avenue
Elgin, Illinois 60120
1-800-774-3360

Resources

This list includes publications to which reference was made in the book and other resources of which we want you to be aware. Those marked with an asterisk (*) are available through The Andrew Center (1-800-774-3360).

> ** A **Study Guide** to accompany **Sharing Living Water** is available from The Andrew Center. The guide provides help for those who want to use **Sharing Living Water** for small group, Sunday school class, administrative group, or retreat study. The guide includes permission to photocopy for use in your church.*

*Andrew Center Staff, *Evangelism: Good News or Bad News?* Elgin: The Andrew Center, 1995. Advocates a passion for evangelism and a passion for peace and justice.

Barna, George, *User Friendly Churches.* Ventura: Regal Books, 1991. Based on careful research, an excellent look at changing the climate in the church.

*Bernhard, Fred and Steve Clapp, *Widening the Welcome of Your Church.* Elgin: The Andrew Center, 1996. Bringing growth and vitality to the church through biblical hospitality.

Bright, Bill, *The Four Spiritual Laws.* San Bernadino: Campus Crusade for Christ. A classic resource on witnessing.

Campolo, Tony and Gordon Aeschliman, *Fifty Ways You Can Share Your Faith.* Downers Grove: InterVarsity Press, 1992. Extremely practical ways you can reach out with Christ's love in actions as well as words.

A Church for the 21st Century. Indianapolis: Center for Congregational Growth and Vitality (Division of Homeland Ministries, The Christian Church). This outstanding video will help churches of any denomination begin dealing with the changes needed for effective outreach.

*Clapp, Steve and Cindy Hollenberg Snider, *Creating Quality in Ministry.* Elgin: The Andrew Center, 1995. Increasing church vitality through an emphasis on quality – includes chapters on both traditional and contemporary worship.

*Clapp, Steve and Kristen Leverton, *Fifty Strategies for Outreach to Teenagers.* Elgin: The Andrew Center, 1996. Strategies to reach teenagers outside the church and inactive youth.

*Clapp, Steve, *Fifty Ways to Reach Young Singles, Couples, and Families*. Elgin: The Andrew Center, 1994. Practical ideas which have been tested in churches around the country.

*Clapp, Steve, *Overcoming Barriers to Church Growth*. Elgin: The Andrew Center, 1994. If you can't get people in your church interested in evangelism, get this book!

*Clapp, Steve and Sam Detwiler, *Peer Evangelism*. Elgin: Brethren Press, 1993. Faith–sharing for teenagers.

*Clapp, Steve and Jerry O. Cook, *Reaching Out Through Christian Education*. Elgin: The Andrew Center, 1994. Packed with practical strategies for reaching out through the Sunday school and other Christian education activities.

Clapp, Steve, *What the Unchurched Have to Teach Us*. Fort Wayne: LifeQuest, 1996. (LifeQuest, 6404 S. Calhoun Street, Fort Wayne, Indiana 46807) Shares information on the focus group study referred to in *Sharing Living Water*.

Easum, William M., *Sacred Cows Make Gourmet Burgers*. Nashville: Abingdon, 1995. Fasten your seat belts, because this book will turn your thinking about the church upside down – and it will disturb you because Easum is right!

Emerging Trends. This publication from the Princeton Religion Research Center (47 Hulfish Street, Suite 215, P.O. Box 389, Princeton, New Jersey 08542) Has excellent reports on the relationship between religious faith and secular culture.

Foster, Richard J., *Celebration of Discipline*. San Francisco: HarperSanFrancisco, 1978, 1988. This well-written book has become an introduction to the classic spiritual disciplines for many people.

Frankl, Viktor E., *Man's Search for Meaning*. New York: Washington Square Press, 1959, 1963. A profound book on his experiences in a concentration camp and the understanding of life he developed as a result.

Glasser, William, *Control Theory*. New York: Harper and Row, 1984. About healthy self-control; not control of others.

Gordon, Sol, *Is There Anything I Can Do?* New York: Delacorte Press, 1994. Not an overtly religious book but filled with marvelous insights on reaching out to people in need.

Hall, Eddy and Gary Morsch, *The Lay Ministry Revolution.* Grand Rapids: Baker, 1995. An outstanding book on empowering lay people for ministry and setting them free to do it.

Kew, Richard and Roger J. White, *New Millennium, New Church.* Boston: Cowley Publications, 1992. (Cowley Publications, 28 Temple Place, Boston, Massachusetts 02111) Especially written from the Episcopal perspective but applicable to most mainline congregations and denominations.

Kramp, John, *Out of Their Faces and into Their Shoes.* Nashville: Broadman and Holman Publishing, 1995. This is the best contemporary book on faith–sharing we've seen except the one you're holding in your hands!

Kübler-Ross, Elisabeth, *On Death and Dying.* New York: Collier Books/Macmillan, 1969. Classic, exceptional, life-changing.

Mandela, Nelson, *Long Walk to Freedom.* New York and Boston: Little Brown and Company, 1994, 1995. Marvelous autobiography by a man who has truly changed history.

McCullough, Donald W., *The Trivialization of God.* Colorado Springs: Navpress, 1995. A very important theological book which should be studied by clergy and laity.

Mead, Loren, *Transforming Congregations for the Future.* Bethesda: The Alban Institute, 1994. An insightful book – helping congregations move into the future. Emphasizes spiritual transformation and institutional change.

Miller, Herb, *Connecting with God.* Nashville: Abingdon, 1994. This is a wonderful book on nurturing the spiritual life of the congregation. You should have a copy.

Miller, Keith, *A Hunger for Healing.* San Francisco: HarperSanFrancisco, 1991. This ground-breaking book shows how the 12-step model relates to the classic spiritual disciplines and can be used to deepen the spiritual life.

*Mundey, Paul, *Change and the Established Congregation.* Elgin: Andrew Center Resources, 1994. An excellent book, based on original research and practical in application.

Net Results. (Cokesbury Subscription Services, 201 Eighth Ave., S, Nashville, TN 37202) A monthly publication edited by Herb Miller and published in cooperation with the evangelism departments of several major denominations. New ideas for evangelism, church vitality, and leadership in each issue.

Neville, Joyce, *How to Share Your Faith without Being Offensive.* New York: Seabury Press, 1983. An excellent treatment of the topic.

Peck, M. Scott, *Further Along the Road Less Traveled.* New York: Simon and Schuster, 1993. A book that has changed lives!

Peck, M. Scott and Marilyn Von Walder, *Gifts for the Journey.* San Francisco: HarperSanFrancisco, 1985, 1995. Many people seem unaware of this beautiful book on the Christian faith. Also available with an audio tape.

Posterski, Donald C., *Reinventing Evangelism.* Downers Grove: InterVarsity Press, 1989. A thought-provoking book which truly speaks to both the Canadian and U.S. church.

Schaller, Lyle E., *Innovations in Ministry.* Nashville: Abingdon, 1994. An outstanding look at emerging models for ministry.

Schaller, Lyle E., *Strategies for Change.* Nashville: Abingdon, 1993. If your church is struggling with change *or* if it needs to be struggling with change, this book will help!

Whan, Norm, *The Phone's For You.* Brea: Church Growth Development. (Church Grown Development, Suite E, 420 W. Lambert, Brea, California 92621) A program for outreach to the community centered on telephone calls.

Williamson, Marianne, *Illuminata.* New York: Random House, 1994. A religious but not distinctly Christian book which will push you to think about faith and life in new ways.